Spas: Planning, Selecting & Installing

Created and Designed by the Editorial Staff of Ortho Books

Project Editor
Alan Ahlstrand

Writer
Ed Scott

Illustrator
Mitzi McCarthy

Principal Photographers
Geoffrey Nilsen
Matthew Yrigoyen

Ortho Books

Publisher
Edward A. Evans

Editorial Director
Christine Jordan

Production Director
Ernie S. Tasaki

Managing Editors
Robert J. Beckstrom
Michael D. Smith
Sally W. Smith

System Manager
Linda M. Bouchard

Product Manager
Richard E. Pile, Jr.

**Marketing Administrative
Assistant**
Daniel Stage

Distribution Specialist
Barbara F. Steadham

Operations Assistant
Georgiann Wright

Technical Consultant
J. A. Crozier, Jr., Ph.D.

Address all inquiries to:
Ortho Books
Chevron Chemical Company
Consumer Products Division
Box 5047
San Ramon, CA 94583-0947

ISBN 0-89721-238-X
Library of Congress Catalog Card Number 90-86166

Chevron Chemical Company
6001 Bollinger Canyon Road, San Ramon, CA 94583

Acknowledgments

Photo Editor
Roberta Spieckerman

Copy Chief
Melinda E. Levine

Editorial Coordinator
Cass Dempsey

Copyeditor
Teresa Castle

Proofreader
Elizabeth von Radics

Indexer
Carolyn McGovern

Editorial Assistants
Deborah Bruner
John Parr
Nancy Patton Wilson-McCune

Composition by
Laurie A. Steele

Layout by
Cynthia Putnam

Production by
Studio 165

Separations by
Color Tech Corp.

Lithographed in the USA by
Webcrafters, Inc.

Photographers
The names below are followed by the page numbers on which their work appears. R=right, C=center, L=left, T=top, B=bottom.

Geoffrey Nilsen Photography: front cover, 1, 3B, 4–5, 6, 8, 9, 10, 12, 14, 17TB, 19, 21, 22, 23, 28, 29TR, 29BL, BR, 30–31, 36, 38, 39, 41, 43, 44–45, 49B, 50, 52, 53, 54, 61, 67, 99–100, back cover

Richard Payne Photography: 97

Mathew Yrigoyen Photography: 72–73, 81, 83, 89, 90, 94, 95, 96

Manufacturers and Designers
Bel Air Spas: 29TR, 99–100, back cover TL
CAL SPAS, a Division of California Acrylic Industries, Inc.: 72–73, 81, 83, 89, 94, 96
Creative Energy Corp.; Novato, Calif.: 27, 44–45, 49B, 77
Tom Dufurrena Architecture: front cover, 6
Cam Fraser Construction: 30–31, 43, back cover TR
Galaxy Spas, Inc.: 7, 21, 23, 53, 61
Debra Gutierrez Interiors: 30–31, 43, back cover TR
Duffy Hurwin Design: front cover, 6
Jacuzzi Inc. Whirlpool Bath— "Athena": 97
Jarvis Architects: 28, 54
Richard Julin & Associates, Landscape Architects: 17T, 29BLR
Kitchen Consultants, Rick Sambol: 30–31, 43, back cover TR
Landscape Fantasies, Gary Gunzenhauser: 1, 4–5, 19, 22
Living Green, Davis Dalbok: front cover, 6
Jim McRory Landscape Design: 41
Magrane/Latker Landscape Design: 12, 14
Native Sons, Jim Zygutis: 21, 23, 53, 61
New Products and Services, Inc.: 8, 9, 17B, 50, 52, 67, back cover BR
Bob Spoor Masonry: 30–31, 43, back cover TR
S.R.W. Construction: front cover, 6
SSI/Sunshine Rooms: 40
Pat Stenger Design: 3B, 36
Jeffrey Stone Associates: 49T, 51

Special Thanks to
James, Lisa, Katelyn, Kyle Bednar
Richard Bell
Roger Budrow
Carol and Rudy Caparros
Susan and Tim Clancy
Andrea Cypress (props)
Yolanda and Conrad Everhardt
Gary Gunzenhauser
Elisheva and Chaim Gur-Arieh
Frank Hoeven
Duffy and Ron Hurwin
MaryEllen Jackson
Glen William Jarvis
John Kasten
Ila and John Kelley
Gerry and Lloyd Lundstrom
Gilliane and Mike McAlister
Patricia and Rudy Meiswinkel
Barbara and Bernard Nestal
Jim Perry
Dick Sallaton
Marion Schwartz
Mitzi Seal
Linda Sommers

Front Cover
Simple elegance and tasteful harmony with natural oceanfront surroundings distinguish this spa.

Title Page
Color, light, sound, fragrance, and a sense of privacy and tranquility reward bathers in this thoughtfully landscaped spa.

Page 3
Top: This natural-looking stone waterfall transforms a custom-built spa into a rocky grotto.
Bottom: This spa room offers a convenient changing area, warm colors, and spacious skylights.

Back Cover
Top left: From an artistic blending of curves to a pleasing integration with the swimming pool, this spa shows the aesthetic and technical results of thoughtful design and planning.

Top right: A special-purpose spa room need be limited only by the designer's imagination.

Bottom left: A well-designed combination of natural and electric lighting enhances the beauty and luxury of this master-bedroom spa.

Bottom right: A few simple additions—a portable spa and privacy lattice enlivened by symmetrically placed hanging plants—turn this small deck into a luxurious oasis.

Spas: Planning, Selecting & Installing

SPAS IN THE OUTDOORS

So you're thinking about adding a spa to your home. This book will guide you through the entire process, from your first look at the various spas in dealers' showrooms through the installation of the spa and on to that first relaxing hot soak.

The first and second chapters cover all aspects of planning for the installation of an outdoor or indoor spa, whether the spa is portable or built-in. Also covered are ways to integrate the spa into the surroundings.

The third chapter of the book discusses the various types of spas, how they are made, what to look for in a quality spa, and how to find a reputable spa dealer. It also covers the purchase contract, financing, and detailed information on the spa support equipment.

The fourth chapter details the techniques of spa installation and provides a step-by-step sequence that will guide you through the process of installing your spa.

The final section contains all of the necessary maintenance procedures to enable you to keep your spa healthful and enjoyable.

The soothing sound of falling water, provided by a waterfall connected to the spa plumbing, can enhance an outdoor spa.

AN OUTDOOR SPA?

The first major decision in installing a spa is whether or not to place it outdoors. The outdoor spa, in the right conditions, will be an improvement to your landscaping and a natural entertainment center.

All the spas, including the swim spas, discussed in this book can be installed either outdoors or indoors. Installing a spa outdoors can add the finishing touch to an attractively landscaped backyard and patio. Any size spa can be integrated into a landscaping, decking, or patio project.

The spa can either be the focal point or it can be played down to simply be part of its surroundings. If you do a lot of outdoor entertaining, such as barbecue parties, the outdoor spa is a natural. Your guests can take a nice hot soak and then enjoy the good food that has been prepared. Also, the sound of bubbling water is always relaxing, even when you're not using the spa; it's like being next to a mountain stream.

Guests may be more relaxed using an outdoor spa than an indoor spa, because they may feel that the surrounding area can get wet without causing any damage. Although an interior room may have been designed for use with a spa, users may feel they shouldn't splash water anywhere, even when getting out of the spa.

If your climate is moderate all year, then the outdoor spa presents no real problems other than slightly higher energy bills during the winter months. An outdoor spa does present a problem if you live in an area where winter temperatures fall below freezing. In cold climates, the spa can be used in winter months, but you must take precautions to protect the spa from damage by freezing and to keep the energy costs to a minimum.

All spas, outdoors and indoors, should be covered for energy conservation when not in use. Covering an outdoor spa when it is not being used also keeps out leaves and debris. Even if the spa is installed aboveground, wind and rain can deposit unwanted debris into uncovered spa water.

Different cover materials and designs provide different degrees of insulation. These are discussed in the third chapter.

An acrylic spa blends harmoniously with a spacious wooden deck to create an oceanfront atmosphere. The table built into the railing corner is just the right size to hold two dinner plates.

The History of Spas

Legend has it that Blalud, the father of King Lear, discovered the therapeutic properties of Bath's hot springs in the ninth century B.C. Roman invaders apparently agreed; they built baths on the site about 50 A.D.

The Saxons—perhaps unclear on the concept—destroyed the Roman baths in 577, but efforts to restore the city eventually succeeded and by 1650, Bath was a famous resort, attracting health-conscious soakers.

At about the same time, the Belgian city which gave us the word *spa* was becoming famous for its mineral springs.

Europeans weren't the only ones to enjoy hot soaking. Archaeologists have found 2,000-year-old baths built into hot springs in Japan. The traditional Japanese *sento*, or public bath, exists today. In North America the 140-degree mineral springs of Hot Springs National Park, in the Ouachita Mountains of Arkansas, had long been enjoyed by Native Americans when Spanish explorer Hernando de Soto discovered the springs in 1541.

Today there are hundreds of health spas and resorts all over the world and thousands of private home spas.

The development that made the modern home spa popular was the Jacuzzi® whirlpool pump, which could simply be placed in an ordinary bathtub. The pump was designed for medical hydrotherapy purposes, but it later became a luxury item for the wealthy. This unique pump produces a blend of air and water that flows around the body, providing a vigorous hydromassage. Later the tub was ergonomically designed to fit the body's contours, complementing the Jacuzzi® pump's effects of relaxing hydrotherapy.

Modern luxury bathtubs are constructed in a manner similar to a spa, with built-in whirlpool and jet pumps. The main difference between a luxury bathtub and a spa is that the tub is filled with fresh water for each use and drained afterwards, whereas the spa has a filtration and heater system that allows the same water to be used continuously for long periods of time.

The wooden hot tub was really the beginning of the spa craze that started in California in the early 1960s using modified half barrels from a winery or whiskey distiller. The wooden hot tub evolved into round or oval vessels made especially for soaking. These were usually made of redwood and could hold up to 10 people. Wooden hot tubs fell out of favor with hot water soakers, however, because they can be difficult to maintain.

Next came the spa, which was made from synthetic materials and seemed to satisfy everyone's hot-water soaking requirements. The spa can be installed either indoors or outdoors and can fit into almost any environment. The spa, as we know it today, has progressed a long way toward greater comfort, material longevity, good support equipment, and affordable price.

Wide, paved decking and a broad lawn complement this spa, manufactured of fiberglass, concrete, and tile.

The larger section of this swim spa can generate an adjustable current to allow exercise swimming in a restricted space. The smaller section can be set to a different temperature for an after-workout soak.

A portable spa and thoughtful decorating turn this small condominium balcony into a pleasant soaking area.

THE SPA LOCATION

A good location is essential to enjoyment of a spa. An ideal location will provide privacy, shelter, and easy access, and it will allow the natural beauty of the spa to enhance the landscaping.

How to Get Started

In planning the spa location, be sure to check your local building code to find out where the spa may be located. Many city and county building codes and ordinances regulate the locations of spas or swimming pools, as well as easements, set-back dimensions from your property line, height of fences, and other factors. It is better to find out where you cannot place the spa at the very beginning than to settle on the perfect place and then be informed that it is not legal.

If you are going to install an in-ground spa, first check to see if there are any underground utilities running through your yard; if so, they must be avoided. If the house has a septic tank, its location must be determined so the spa will not be located close to it.

If you are adding a spa to a yard that is already landscaped or has an existing deck, the site selection is less complicated. You can easily visualize the view from the spa with the landscaping or deck already in place. If you are starting with a bare yard or are going to completely redo the yard, your planning will be more complicated. To begin,

A low stone wall gives a built-in look to a portable spa.

Landscaping Plan

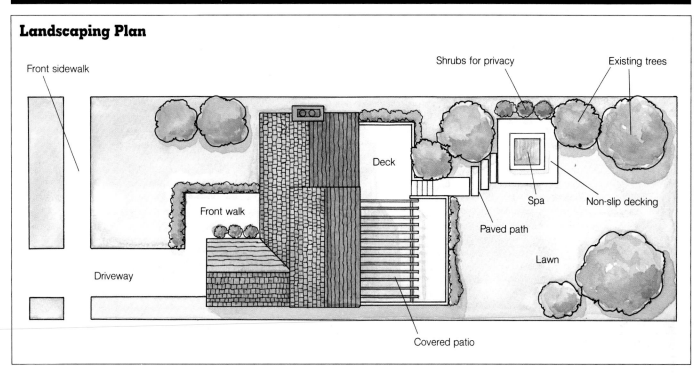

Front sidewalk

Shrubs for privacy

Existing trees

Deck

Spa

Non-slip decking

Paved path

Front walk

Lawn

Driveway

Covered patio

walk around the backyard or side yard and look over the surroundings. If the yard is going to be completely landscaped, try to visualize the project when it is completed. Take a patio chair and sit down at various locations in the yard that could be possible sites for the spa. Look around in all directions, check out the existing view, and try to visualize what the view will be like when the landscaping is done. If the spa is to be installed at ground level, spread out a blanket and lie on the ground to get the correct perspective on the view. If you have a Polaroid camera, take some pictures from each proposed spa site so that you can compare one with the other.

If nearby trees shed leaves and needles or have blossoms or pods that fall, don't locate the spa close to them. These trees will create debris that must be cleaned out of the spa frequently. The trees may be

beautiful and may offer subtle shade, but if they are mess makers, avoid putting the spa near them.

If you live in an area where it snows in the winter, don't locate the spa under the roof eaves. When the snow starts to melt and slides off the roof, it will end up in the spa and could damage the spa and the spa cover.

Hot soaking, other than at party time, is usually a private affair. Investigate the neighbors' views of your yard, especially if you choose to soak au naturel. Don't rule out any location just because of the lack of privacy, however, because this problem can be solved by trees, screening, fencing, an overhead structure, or a gazebo. You may want the spa close to the house for quick access, or you may want it farther away from the house in its own quiet environment.

Finding the correct location is very important, so don't make a hasty decision. Come up with several possible locations and observe each one during morning, noon, afternoon, and evening hours. A location that is quite suitable during the daytime may not lend itself to night use. Continue to check the locations until you find the one that best suits your specific purposes and with which you are most comfortable. Once you have committed to a site location, you should stick with it. The site can be changed after construction starts, but that could prove very expensive, especially once the yard has already been graded.

A Plan View Drawing

Now is the time to make a plan view drawing of your yard, the house, and any existing garden structures. You will need a couple of 50- to 100-foot measuring

tapes, some graph paper, a circle template, landscape template, a triangle, an architect's scale, drafting or masking tape, a pencil sharpener, and an eraser. A convenient scale for this drawing is ⅛ or ¼ inch to 1 foot. First, precisely measure the outline of the yard (property lines), including the fences and the back portion of the house in relation to the yard, and use these dimensions to make a line drawing on the graph paper. Be sure to include all nonmovable structures in the yard, such as gazebos or garden sheds. Use the back fence or the back surface of the house as a baseline for all further measurements. This drawing can be used to finalize the spa location; it can also be used for planning your landscaping and plotting the path of the sun through the yard.

Once you have settled on the spa location, and the basic

landscape and decking are planned, you may want to consult with a landscape architect for an expert opinion on what you have decided to do. Most landscape architects work on an hourly basis for initial designs, so spend some time with them and tap their fund of knowledge before taking on such a large project. They can give you a lot of pointers from past experience on what to do as well as what not to do.

Existing Grade of the Yard

The ideal placement for the spa is on level ground. If the yard is level, or close to level, little effort will be required to prepare the site for the spa installation. The levelness of the site can be checked with a special tool called a line level. This is a bubble level that is attached to a strong string. Use the line level to check the site in both the north-to-south direction and the east-to-west direction.

A minor deviation from level in either direction can be changed by moving the dirt by hand with a shovel. If the site is sloped in one or both directions, it is best to call in an excavation contractor to level the site. If a lot of cutting and filling of the ground is required, the contractor will have the heavy machinery necessary to do the job. Also, after the ground is moved around, a retaining wall must be added to support the newly moved dirt.

Do not choose a spa site in an area where there is a natural drainage channel through the yard for rain runoff or landscape watering. This is especially true if the spa is going to be installed permanently in the ground because you will not want runoff water and dirt flowing into the spa.

A stone retaining wall—barely visible behind plantings—secures the slope above this Rovel® thermoplastic swim spa.

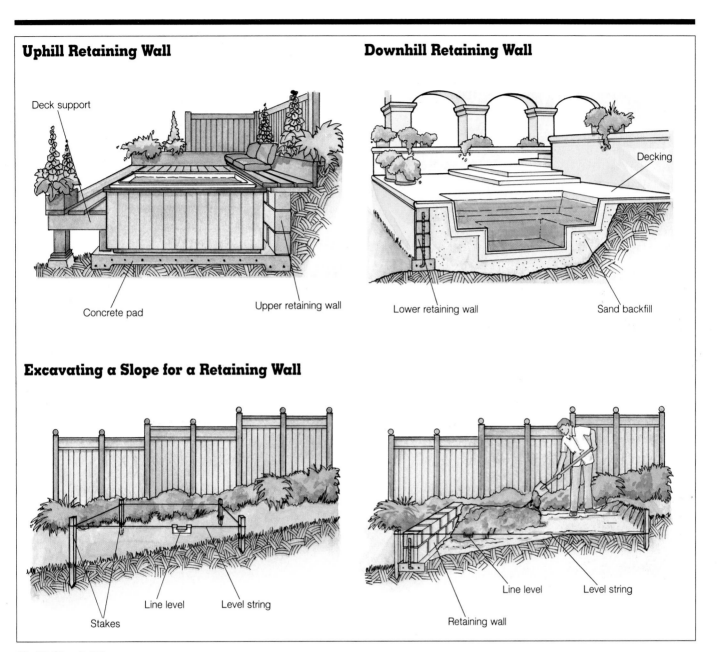

Uphill Retaining Wall

Deck support

Concrete pad

Upper retaining wall

Downhill Retaining Wall

Decking

Lower retaining wall

Sand backfill

Excavating a Slope for a Retaining Wall

Line level

Level string

Stakes

Line level

Level string

Retaining wall

Soil Stability and Composition

If you are going to install a spa into a level or nearly level site, soil stability and soil composition will not be very important. If the spa site requires a lot of excavation or the spa is going to be installed on a hillside or severe slope, soil stability and composition should be determined by a qualified civil engineer. Once the spa is installed and filled with water, it becomes a heavy body that could move downhill if the soil is unstable.

Soil consists of uncemented or weakly cemented mineral particles that have been formed by the weathering or breaking up of rocks. These particles have voids between them that are filled with air or water. Dirt that has been in place for a long time and has not been moved is called residual soil and is usually stable. Soil that has been graded or moved from its original location is referred to as transported soil; it is less stable and must be retained by a wall or similar structure.

Water drainage must also be considered, especially if dirt was moved to accommodate the spa. If the natural drainage through the yard has been interrupted by the excavation process, drainage pipes or channels must be installed through the area to allow the natural flow of water to continue without damage to the newly moved dirt. If drainage is not provided, rain runoff will erode the newly moved dirt and could undermine the spa and any surrounding deck.

To establish the description and classification of the soil, tests must be performed in a laboratory by trained personnel, but some experienced civil engineers can determine soil condition at the job site without special equipment. Soils fall into different categories (for example, sand, gravel, silt, clay, organic matter) and each type has its strengths and weaknesses. Don't take a chance by installing a spa on a hillside without having the soil thoroughly analyzed by a qualified professional.

Exposure to Sun and Shade

If the spa will often be used during the daytime, then its location should be planned in relation to the path of the sun through the yard. A south-facing spa will receive the most sunlight; a northern exposure will receive the least. The spa should face eastward for morning sun or westward for late afternoon exposure. A southern exposure can add several weeks of sunlight to a spa by allowing sun exposure earlier in the spring and later in the fall. Sun-loving landscape planting surrounding the spa will grow better with a southern or western exposure.

Remember that the sun's position in the sky moves during the year. In the winter months the sun is in the southern portion of the sky; it moves northward as summer approaches. This moves the path of the sun on the ground approximately 10 to 15 feet.

Selecting a spa location with good sun exposure is usually preferable, but if you live in a

A custom-built spa nestles in the end of this formal reflecting pool.

very warm area, like the desert, the midday sun may be too hot, making it uncomfortable to use the spa. In locations such as this, you can still consider a southern exposure, but you may need selective shade with screening or a movable overhead cover.

Sun exposure is very important for the spa location, but shade must also be considered. Shade caused by neighboring houses, an adjacent tree, a hillside, or fencing can cut down on the use of the spa.

Charting the Sun's Path in Your Yard

Charting the path of the sun through the yard can be accomplished in one day. You will need 50 to 60 or more wooden stakes 18 to 24 inches long, some string, and 12 paper shipping tags. The stakes will be placed in the ground where the shadow line changes direction; the string will go from stake to stake to indicate the shadow line; the tags will be used to indicate the time of day at which each string line was placed on the ground.

Note the date, since the angle of the sun changes with the seasons. If your planning schedule allows it, take the measurement monthly for several months. If not, you can estimate the change in the shadow line during the year.

Start in the morning when the sun first comes up and work throughout the day, every hour, until dusk. Do this on a day when you expect the sun to be out all day.

You will be making hourly outlines of the sun-to-shadow

line as it crosses the surface of the yard. You won't have to follow the shadow line exactly; it's fine to round off the shape between the stakes and cut a few corners, otherwise you would need 100 or more stakes. Each of the shadow lines includes the shadow outline of all structures and plants that cast a shadow onto your property.

Since the shade outlines—and therefore the strings—may overlap as they cross the ground, start out by positioning the string used on the first series of stakes near ground level. With each new hourly series of stakes and string, position the string slightly higher on the stakes as you progress through the day.

Start about 6 a.m. at one side of the yard and place the first stake in the ground at the beginning of the shadow line. Tie the string to the stake, then follow the shadow line on the ground with the string until it makes a change in direction. At that point drive in another stake, pull the string tight, and wrap it around the second stake. Move on with the string again, following the shadow line on the ground, until the shadow line makes another change in direction. Again, drive in another stake and wrap the string around it. Continue with the string and stakes until you have crossed the entire yard. At the last stake for the 6 a.m. shadow line, attach one of the shipping tags and mark the time of day on it (that is, 6 a.m.).

Repeat this procedure every hour on the hour and tag the last stake of each shadow line

Daily Shade Pattern Changes

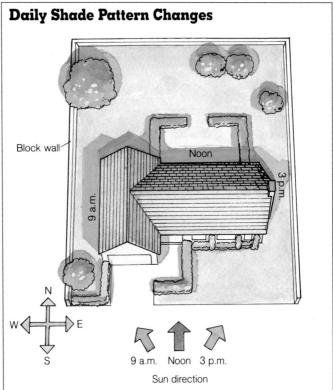

Seasonal Changes in the Sun's Path

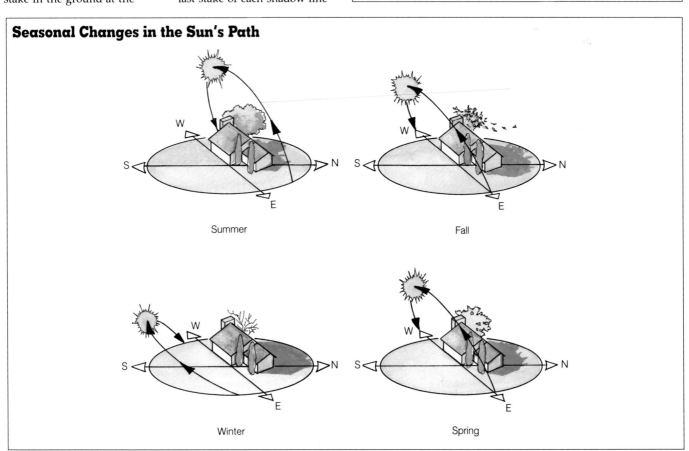

Summer

Fall

Winter

Spring

Wind Protection

Straight lattice fence

Straight solid fence

Solid fence; top tilted inward

Solid fence; top tilted outward

with the time of day. At the end of the day you will have plotted the sun-to-shadow line across the entire yard. You will probably be surprised to find where the sun does and does not shine in the yard. All of this must now be plotted on paper for future planning.

Measure each shadow line and draw it on a piece of tracing paper, superimposed on the plan view drawing that was described earlier (page 11).

Label each line to show the time of day it represents; you may want to use different colored pencils or different types of lines (for example, broken, dotted, or dashed lines) to differentiate the individual shadow lines. You will need to be able to identify each of the shadow lines separately to accurately chart the movement of the sun across your yard.

Wind Protection

Some yards are protected from prevailing winds by structures or trees, while in other yards the wind is always present and must be considered carefully when planning the spa location. In some regions the wind shifts during different times of the year; this must be considered if the spa will be used year around. Not only will the wind tend to chill people using the spa, it will also cool off the

spa water, which means the water heater will have to work harder to maintain the desired water temperature. The wind can be blocked, if necessary, but it is best to find a location free of wind currents. Northern exposure should be avoided, if possible, especially if you live in a cold climate or where cool northerly winds are common.

Wind will also have an effect on the performance of the spa skimmer, because the wind can cause surface currents. If you are unable to control the wind at your spa site completely, locate the skimmer downwind so the wind will blow the debris into the skimmer—not away from it.

If the desired spa location has a wind problem, it can be solved by screening or plantings. If you want a semiopen screen, consider redwood lattice, bamboo, shade cloth, or canvas panels. Flats of redwood lattice or pre-assembled lattice panels are inexpensive and attractive. Redwood lattice is lightweight, so it doesn't need a heavy support frame. The latticework can be left in its natural color, or it can be stained or painted.

Redwood lattice panels are readily available and can be installed in various ways. The panels can be mounted permanently, or they can be hinged or placed in tracks so they can be moved to open or close off the spa area. If the lattice panels are permanent, decorative vines can be planted at the base of the panels and then trained on them. Vinyl lattice, which is smoother than wood and comes in colors, is also available.

Bamboo can also be used for screening. However, bamboo does limit the appearance of the spa and its surroundings because it usually indicates a Polynesian motif.

Two other materials to consider are polypropylene-mesh shade cloth, used mainly for patio covers, and canvas. The shade cloth is available in various densities that block 30 to 90 percent of the sunlight. It is available only in dark green or black. It can be used to block wind in a similar manner. Canvas is solid and will not allow any breeze to flow through it,

but it is available in many different colors. Both shade cloth and canvas can be permanently mounted into wooden frames or installed so the cloth can be rolled up to allow in sunlight and breezes.

If the wind is to be blocked off all the time, solid panels are best. For an unobstructed view, you can use transparent-plastic or tempered-glass panels in a wooden or masonry support structure. If the view is not important, almost any type of material, such as fiberglass or plywood, can be used for a screen. This screening can also be part of any required fencing, which will prevent you from having to build two separate structures.

Shower and Changing Room

If the spa is not located near a house bathroom, a separate shower and changing room can be built near the spa.

A shower and changing room close to the spa will reduce wet foot traffic into the house and can double as a place to clean up after working in the yard. This will also make it easy for soakers to shower. Showering with soap and hot water before using the spa will keep the water clean longer.

The changing room should contain a separate shower area, a sink and mirror, a bench to sit on while changing clothes, towel racks, and a place to hang or lay clothes. You may even consider purchasing small bottles of shampoo and a supply of soap for your guests. If you do a lot of entertaining, you may want to add a toilet to the room as well.

A shower and changing room in a separate building provide luxury and convenience.

Privacy lattice, with the top portion leaning inward, provides effective wind protection while screening the view from a neighbor's home.

LANDSCAPING

Whether it conceals the spa or highlights it, landscaping is the key artistic element in installing an outdoor spa. Landscaping can emphasize a location's good points or counteract its flaws.

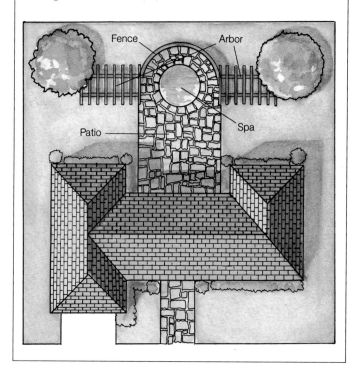

Sample Plan View

Fence — Arbor — Spa — Patio

Plan Development

In turning your backyard into a more pleasant environment, do not limit yourself to plants, shrubs, and trees; also consider decks, pathways, screens, fences, overhead structures, lighting, and gazebos. These should work together to create a comfortable and relaxing atmosphere at all times, not just when the spa is in use.

You will want to integrate the landscaping with the spa, but you may not want to make the spa the center of interest because it will not be in use all the time. The landscaping elements should be able to stand alone and be pleasing by themselves.

If the spa is an in-ground type, it can also double as a reflective pool or a pond when not in use. If the spa is equipped with a waterfall, the cascading water will lend a soothing sound during a quiet outdoor dinner party. Note that running the air blowers or hydrojets to create calming white noise may drastically lower the water temperature. After the party is over, be sure to turn off the jets or blowers and install the cover to maintain the water temperature and keep out debris.

The plan-view scale drawing of your yard and house, described earlier, can be used to plan your landscaping. If they aren't already drawn in, add the location of existing water spigots, electrical outlets, decks, paths, trees, and any parts of the existing landscape that are to remain unchanged. Don't draw in any items that you plan to remove. Place a piece of tracing paper over the plan view drawing and start sketching where you think the various parts and pieces of new landscaping will look best. Mark areas that may need to be screened off to block a neighbor's view of the spa or to hide unsightly objects, such as power poles. Indicate the wind direction and, if you have not already done so, the sunshine and shadow lines throughout the yard. Include all the new items you plan to install, such as the spa, and perhaps a built-in barbecue, an entertainment area, decks, flower beds, or a children's play area. Come up with as many possible designs as you can. This is time well spent because it doesn't cost any money to move a tree on a piece of paper, but once in the ground it's a different story. Sketch out a number of ideas and set them aside; come back to them in a couple of days and look them over again. At this time you may come up with a completely different idea or you may settle on a design that you liked before.

Once you have the final idea on the scale drawing, try it out in full size. Pick out one item on the scale drawing and visualize it in the yard. Doing this will probably result in a few changes—some minor, some major.

A more precise way to visualize your spa and its surrounding is to outline the plan on your yard using gypsum purchased from a hardware store. This is the white powder used for marking lines on the grass fields at sporting events. It will not harm any existing grass. Transfer the outline dimensions for the new large components, such as the spa, deck, shower room, and footpaths, onto the ground and make an outline of each item with the gypsum powder. After all items are marked on the ground with the gypsum, walk around the yard from the deck to the shower room to the spa. Does this layout work? Is it easy to get from one place to another? If you are unhappy with the plan, use a garden hose to water the gypsum line into the grass or sweep it away with a broom. Move the spa, or footpath, or whatever is wrong, then add the new lines and walk around again to see how the elements relate to each other. Take a patio chair and set it on the imaginary deck and sample the view. Try different variations until you are happy with the final layout. Once things are finalized, make the changes on the plan view drawing.

Time, imagination, and effort have turned this simple fiberglass spa into a serene wooded glen.

Shelter From the Elements

One of the main reasons for landscaping is to create a relaxing environment, free of all elements that would annoy you and your guests. Wind, hot sun, and even noise from a neighbor's yard or the street can be a real problem when you're trying to design a quiet and comfortable spa environment. Sheltering can be accomplished with artificial screens, and it can also be achieved with natural plantings. Hedges, flowers, shrubs, and trees provide a soft, natural feeling that can also add color at different times of the year. You can achieve a formal or rustic feeling by using different types of foliage. A screen of hedges can be sheared for a formal look or left unsheared to achieve a softer, rustic appearance.

If you want the screening all year, choose plants that are evergreen, since they will not drop their foliage in the winter.

In some areas you may want the screening to lose its leaves so the winter sunlight can pass through the bare branches, creating an interesting sunlight-and-shadow pattern. If this is desirable, choose deciduous plants that go bare in the winter and produce fresh new foliage in the spring. Don't place deciduous plants close to the spa because the debris they create when they lose their foliage can litter the spa.

An interesting effect can be achieved by using a combination of both types of planting in one area. This will create a solid wall of foliage during the summer, when the spa is more likely to be used, then offer a more open feeling in winter when the deciduous plants lose their foliage.

All plants or trees need not be planted in the ground. A pleasing effect can be achieved with shrubs, plants, and small trees in different types of movable containers. Clay pots and wooden planters are attractive and can be moved to various parts of the yard to achieve different visual effects. If you choose to do some container planting, make sure the plants you choose are well suited for this type of gardening. Some plants and trees will thrive in a container, but others will simply become root bound and die, or never really grow.

Be sure to choose plantings that do not have thorns or any type of sharp burrs that may harm eyes, bare feet, or bodies, and also make sure they do not have blossoms that would attract bees.

The Correct Type of Plants

Many factors are involved in selecting plants. Individual plants should be considered in conjunction with the rest of the landscaping. Plantings must also be appropriate for the local climate. Choose plants that will thrive. If you try to grow something that is not appropriate for your climate, it will probably never reach its peak in appearance and size; it may not even survive.

Plants, shrubs, and trees all have different water needs as well as different sun or shade requirements. Be sure to choose plants that are compatible. Don't plant a water-loving plant under a tree that requires little or no water; you will end up losing one or both of them.

If you live in an area where dry spells frequently occur, concentrate on plantings that are drought-resistant. You may want to consider a rock garden as well as the addition of fairly large boulders. Among the rocks, you can grow many types of vegetation that survive on very little water. Ortho gardening books and your local nursery will provide suggestions on plantings that require minimal watering.

Consider the amount of upkeep each plant requires. If you don't want to spend every weekend working in the yard, choose low-maintenance plantings. Many beautiful plants require little or no maintenance other than some routine watering and fertilizer at the correct time of year. Other plants require pruning, watering, special fertilizer, and fumigation

against insects in order to look healthy throughout the year. You may want to design a yard using different evergreens that require little upkeep, then add small pocket gardens where bright seasonal flowers can be planted. When these flowers are past their prime, remove them and replant the area with another type of flower suited to the season.

When choosing the landscaping material that is adjacent to the spa, remember to use plantings that do not generate leaves, seeds, needles, pods, dead blossoms, and debris that will end up in the spa water. If you love a certain plant that fits into this category and you want to plant it close to the spa, place it on the downwind side of the spa so any debris will be blown away from the spa and not into it.

One very important point to remember in landscaping is that some plants are dangerous. Some have thorns or sharp burrs; others are poisonous.

Poisonous plants should not be used, especially if children play in your yard. This is a partial list of poisonous plants, berries, and nuts, provided by the Los Angeles Arboretum: azalea, bird-of-paradise, castorbean, foxglove, holly berries, horse chestnuts, hydrangea, ivy berries, lantana, oleander, and rhododendron. Consult a local nursery, arboretum, or poison control center for additional information regarding poisonous plants that are not listed here.

DECKS AND DECKING

The immediate surroundings of a spa make a lasting impression on bathers. An attractive decking surface, or a wooden deck smoothly integrated with the spa and landscaping, will make soaking a pleasing visual experience.

Practical Considerations

A deck is an elevated wooden structure. Decking is the surface that surrounds a spa (or swimming pool) and separates it from the landscaping or deck.

There are two reasons to install a deck or decking surface around the spa. The first is safety. The area around the spa will get wet as people get into and out of the spa. The surface should be as nonslippery as possible to lessen the possibility of accidents. The second reason is to have an area that can easily be kept clean so people will not track dirt and debris into the spa. When walking through the backyard to an outdoor spa, even on a walkway, you are bound to pick up some dirt on your shoes or feet. Upon reaching the deck or decking surface, you should clean the dirt off before entering the spa. You might also consider placing a piece of indoor/outdoor carpeting on the floor area where people step out of the spa.

Decking can be built with materials such as bricks, concrete, ceramic tile, or an epoxy-based poured aggregate. Decking can also be made with natural materials, such as flagstone, rocks, or stones. These different materials can be used by themselves, or they can be combined with each other to make a pleasing and safe perimeter for your spa.

The decking surface must be able to withstand water and cannot be slippery when wet. The surface should be easy to maintain. If you live in an area where the temperature changes are drastic, the decking materials must be able to withstand the winter freeze and the summer heat without cracking or sustaining any other type of damage. Combining the correct types of decking material will enhance the spa and coordinate it with surrounding landscaping. The decking should be beautiful, but it must also be comfortable to walk on in bare feet. Any spilled water from the spa must drain off easily. If water is allowed to run back into the spa, it will usually carry debris with it.

The typical drain slope of ¼ inch drop per foot applies to wood, concrete, and natural stone construction. This slope is usually sufficient, but be sure to check your local building code for specific regulations in your area.

A ¼-inch-per-foot drain slope is barely noticeable and is easy to walk on. Do not increase the drain slope beyond code specifications because the

The boards on each level of this deck are laid in different directions to increase safety as well as to create a visually pleasing contrast.

surface may become difficult to walk on and may even cause someone to slip.

Decks can be classified into two categories: attached and freestanding. Attached decks are connected to an existing structure such as the house or garage; freestanding decks are completely self-supporting. Within these categories there are many variations. If your yard is large enough, you may choose to have both types. The main deck can be attached to the house, with the deck entryway from the family room, for instance, and the freestanding deck can surround the spa and be joined to the other decks by a friendly footpath. The possibilities are limited only by the size of your yard and budget.

In most locations, a building permit will be required to construct a deck and may be included in the spa permit.

Consult your local building department for details. For more information on deck construction, see Ortho's book *How to Design & Build Decks & Patios.*

Wood for a Deck

When you select the type of wood for a deck, you need to consider availability, durability, structural requirements, appearance, and cost. If the deck will be the focal point in part of the yard, the appearance of the wood should be the primary concern.

Heart-grade redwood and cedar are the woods used most often in deck construction because both have a nice appearance and are resistant to rot, decay, and insect infestation. Redwood is usually more expensive, but other types of wood can be used if they are pressure treated. Most large

lumberyards carry pressure-treated wood, which is available in brown or green. If you are unable to find the wood of your choice that has been pressure treated you can treat the wood yourself with an approved wood preservative. Preserving the wood yourself is not as effective as pressure treatment, but is better than not treating the wood at all. The best way to apply the preservative is to soak the wood in it overnight. If this is not possible, it can be applied by brush, roller, or spray gun. Be sure to read and follow all label precautions when applying a preservative.

Different types of wood take on a different appearance after they have been in use and have been exposed to the elements. Untreated wood changes color with prolonged exposure. Untreated redwood will usually turn very dark with age; cedar will turn a silvery gray. Most treated wood will retain its original treated color and may soften in hue with age. If you are not sure what the wood will look like after exposure, look at some decks in your neighborhood that are made from different types of wood and ones that have been treated differently. This can assist you in making the final decision on which wood to use.

The grain pattern also affects the appearance of the wood. Wood grain is either flat (a wide and curvy pattern) or vertical (a straight, parallel pattern). By looking at the end of the piece of wood, you can tell which way the grain is traveling through it. If the deck is going to be small, choose a vertical grain with a minimal amount of knots. Knot-free clear wood is best.

Wood is graded by an independent grading agency according to its strength and its appearance. The grading stamp will specify which independent agency graded the wood, which mill produced it, the quality of the board, how dry it is, and the wood species (for example, fir). The grade is usually stamped on one side of the piece of wood. There are two major grades of wood or lumber: select and common. Select lumber is used for finish carpentry, such as cabinets and interior projects, and would not be used in deck construction. Common lumber is used for exterior construction.

Common lumber is classified in four categories: select structural, structural joists and planks, light framing, and stud grade. Within these categories there is also grading from No. 1 to No. 4.

Grade No. 1 of select structural lumber is recommended for attractive appearance as well as strength and stiffness. No. 2 is less desirable in appearance but retains high strength. No. 3 is recommended for general construction that does not require the high strength necessary for floor joists and rafters. Structural joists and planks are graded in a manner similar to select structural lumber.

Light framing lumber is classified as construction grade, standard grade, and utility. Construction grade is the best, as it is strong and stiff with minimal knots. Standard grade is close to construction grade but has more knots and less strength. Utility grade is for light framing and is usually

These timber steps provide a nonslip surface.

Lumber Grading Stamp

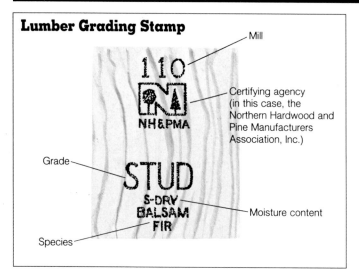

110

NH&PMA

Mill

Certifying agency
(in this case, the
Northern Hardwood and
Pine Manufacturers
Association, Inc.)

Grade

STUD

S-DRY
BALSAM
FIR

Moisture content

Species

weak, has a lot of knots, and is not recommended for any load-bearing applications.

Stud grade lumber is used mainly for studs in residential wall framing. It is usually quite straight and sturdy and is normally available in lengths of 10 feet or less.

To keep the wooden support structure dry and strong, there must be ample air circulation under the deck. This is especially true for a deck that is built close to the ground. Any spa water or landscape water that collects under the deck must be able to drain out or evaporate. If the water is allowed to remain, it will create musty stagnant air and will provide a breeding ground for insects like mosquitoes. It will also lead to dry rot and termite infestation in the wood.

Single or Multilevel Decks

When you plan deck ideas, try to visualize both single-level and multilevel decks. If you plan to install an aboveground spa or use a portable spa, a multilevel deck can produce

the best results in integrating the spa into the rest of the landscaping.

If your yard is level, or nearly so, a single-level deck will probably create a pleasing atmosphere to surround an in-ground spa; it is also the least expensive and the easiest to build. You don't have to restrict the outer shape of the deck to a square or rectangle; a more interesting effect can be achieved by using a variety of outlines. The deck can be built around large rocks in the yard and can even surround an existing tree or group of trees. If you build a deck around a tree, be sure to allow room for the tree to grow and also room for tree movement in the wind.

A multilevel deck is ideal for a sloped yard. The different deck levels can follow the ground surface and be connected by stairways. This is preferable to building a large single-level deck that juts out into space with a very sharp drop from the deck surface to

the ground below. Multilevel decks offer greater visual interest than single-level decks due to the intersecting planes and angles. These levels will create separate entertaining and seating areas and will also provide handy storage areas under the different layers. In building a multilevel deck, change the direction of the deck boards at each level to add visual appeal and to call attention to the surface-level change for safety.

Deck Supports

The deck must be supported correctly to ensure a steady structure, especially if the deck is elevated above the ground by some distance. Don't overbuild the deck support structure, but also don't build a deck that shakes or moves slightly when someone walks on it. When in doubt, build it a little stronger than necessary. The design of

the deck and its support structure must be approved by your local building department if a permit is required. The local building code will give you the specifications for the size of footings and supports, the distance between spans, and the size of lumber for all parts of the deck. Some lumberyards provide charts showing the recommended spans between the different parts of the deck and also the recommended size of lumber for the various support components, including the footings.

The deck support structure starts with precast concrete piers or poured concrete footings in the ground. These provide stability and also keep the beams off the ground to protect them from moisture and termites. Posts are attached to the tops of the footings, then the beams are placed on top of the posts and attached to them.

Fiberglass, concrete, and tile construction gives a custom look to a manufactured spa.

Section View of a Multilevel Deck

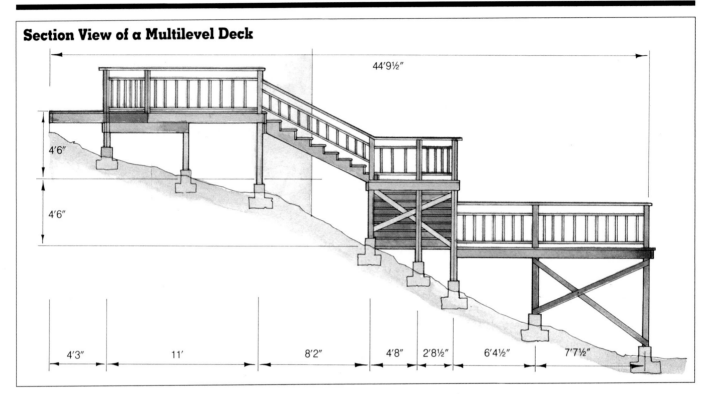

44'9½"

4'6"

4'6"

4'3"　　11'　　8'2"　　4'8"　2'8½"　6'4½"　　7'7½"

The deck joists are attached to the beams, and the decking material is nailed to the joists.

In some cases this is not possible; in such a situation you can use metal joist hangers to attach the joists to the beams. These metal fasteners come in different dimensions to accept different sizes of lumber and are available from major hardware stores and lumberyards. This type of construction is usually acceptable to local building departments, but it should be verified first.

Calculating the Weight of the Spa

If the spa will be placed on the deck surface instead of on the ground, that portion of the deck must be able to support the spa when it is filled with water and people. You must calculate the weight per square foot that will be transferred to

the deck surface. For example, if the spa weighs 8,500 pounds when filled with water and people, and the bottom surface area of the spa is 35 square feet, then divide the spa weight of 8,500 pounds by the 35-square-foot area of the spa. This equals approximately 243 pounds per square foot.

Spa literature often includes the weight of the spa when filled with water and people. Otherwise, you can make the calculation yourself. Water weighs about 8 pounds per gallon. Multiply the number of gallons by 8 to find the total pounds of water. Add weight for the maximum number of people who will occupy the spa at the same time, then add the weight of the spa itself. Once the total weight is established, refer to your local building

code to determine the substructure requirements.

The substructure required directly under the spa must be stronger than that required for the remainder of the deck. Don't overbuild the entire deck just to accept the spa weight; concentrate the stronger substructure directly below the spa, and build the rest of the deck to support the normal deck load.

Stairs

Stairs leading to the spa or to different levels of a deck should be clearly defined for safety as well as aesthetics. Stairs are almost always a safety concern, no matter where they are placed. All stair areas should be illuminated for safe nighttime use.

Stairs consist of treads (the horizontal part), risers (the vertical part), and stringers,

which support the treads and risers on each side. The stringer is usually made of 2 by 12s so there is enough material remaining after the cutouts are removed for the treads and risers. For outdoor applications, the risers can be eliminated to achieve an airy, open feeling, provided the area under the stairs is well maintained.

Stairs require careful consideration so they will be safe to use. They must be strong enough to carry the weight of people, the tread pattern must be uniform so the treads and risers have the same dimensions throughout the set of stairs, and they must not be slippery.

To maintain a consistent appearance, the stair treads and risers should be made from the same type and size of lumber used for the deck surface. If you want the stairs to have a

Stair Construction

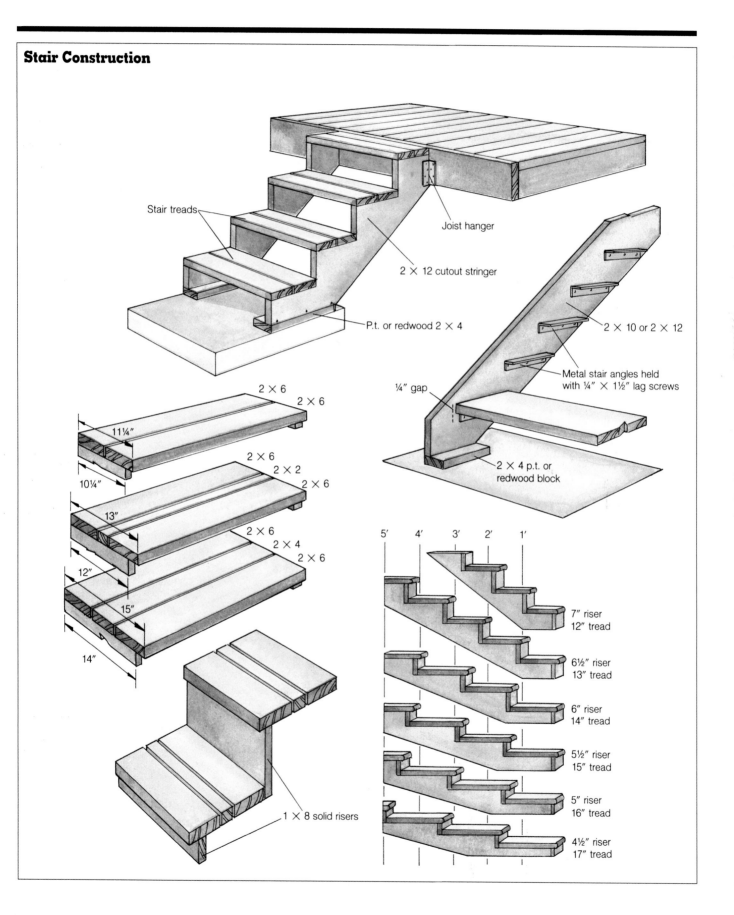

Stair treads

Joist hanger

2 × 12 cutout stringer

P.t. or redwood 2 × 4

2 × 6
2 × 6
11¼"
10¼"
2 × 6
2 × 2
2 × 6
13"
2 × 6
2 × 4
2 × 6
12"
15"
14"

1 × 8 solid risers

2 × 10 or 2 × 12

¼" gap

Metal stair angles held
with ¼" × 1½" lag screws

2 × 4 p.t. or
redwood block

5'   4'   3'   2'   1'

7" riser
12" tread

6½" riser
13" tread

6" riser
14" tread

5½" riser
15" tread

5" riser
16" tread

4½" riser
17" tread

Railing Details

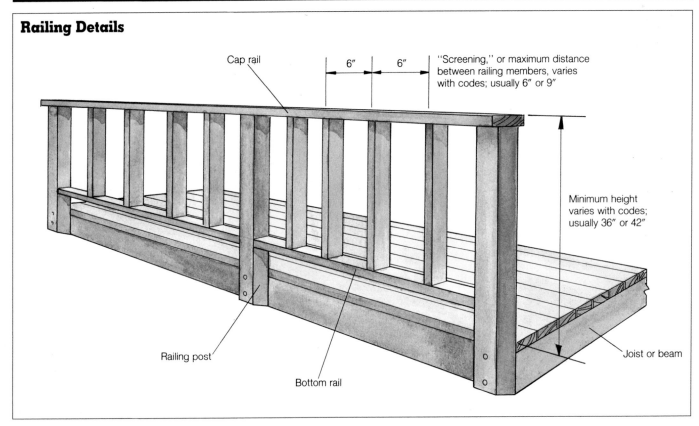

Cap rail

6″   6″

"Screening," or maximum distance between railing members, varies with codes; usually 6″ or 9″

Minimum height varies with codes; usually 36″ or 42″

Railing post

Bottom rail

Joist or beam

different appearance from the deck, use a material other than wood, or use a wood whose appearance is completely different from that used on the deck. Don't use something only slightly different in appearance, as it will look like a mismatch or mistake.

The stairs must have a constant ratio of riser to tread for safety. The first step can be slightly lower or higher than the remaining risers, but the height of the rest of the steps should be consistent. If there is a series of multilevel decks connected by various sets of stairs, the ratio should remain the same throughout all sets. The stair ratio used with outdoor decks can vary from the 7-inch rise and 11-inch tread normally

accepted for interior staircases. A ratio of 6 inches to 12 inches can be used for stair construction so the stairs can be made from 2 by 6s, using one 2 by 6 for the riser and two 2 by 6s for the tread. This ratio is too low and wide for house interiors, but it provides a more stable footing on deck stairs. The leading edge of the tread should overlap the riser below by about ½ inch to create a shadow line which helps define the next step. The upper ends of the stringers should be attached to the deck header with a 2 by 12 joist hanger on each side. The lower ends of the stringers can be attached to the lower deck or placed on concrete, bricks, or pressure-treated lumber specified for ground contact. Never rest the lower ends of the stringers on bare ground; it is unstable, and

the wood will absorb ground moisture, leading to rot and termite infestation.

Railings

All raised decks and stairways should be protected by railings for safety as well as appearance. Many local building codes require railings for stairs when there are a certain number of stairs in a set. Whether they are required or not, railings should be installed. In addition to increasing safety, the railings will help integrate multilevel decks and stairways into a cohesive unit. Depending on local building code requirements, the top railing should be about 36 to 42 inches above the deck surface, 30 to 33 inches above steps.

Railings can be constructed from many different materials, but they should tie in with those used on the deck and stairs. On a deck located close to the ground, the railing can be made from strong rope strung between posts because little protection is needed in this situation. If the deck and stairs are elevated higher above the ground, then the railing and the horizontal or vertical railing members must be designed to prevent children from falling through the balusters. Most areas require a 36-inch railing height; some require a 42-inch height. Screening (the maximum distance between railing members) is 6 inches in most areas, and 9 inches in some areas. The balusters must provide a lateral resistance of 15 pounds per foot of length.

Many types of materials can be used to fill in the area between the top rail and the deck or stair surface. If you don't want to block a good view, you can use a wire mesh with large openings called hardware cloth. Other materials include redwood lattice, vertical or horizontal wood strips, or sheets of clear plastic or tempered glass. If the view is not important, the area can be filled in solidly with wood siding.

The railings and balusters can be very decorative or very simple, depending on the design of the decks and stairs. Remember that the handrail will be used frequently and, therefore, must be smooth and free of splinters at all times.

Benches

When you design the decks and railings, you should consider adding benches at the same time. The benches can then be integrated into the design of the deck. By building the benches at the outer edge of the deck, you will end up with more usable deck space.

To make sure the benches are comfortable to sit and lounge on, they should be 15 to 18 inches above the deck surface and about 15 inches deep. In some areas of the deck, the top portion of the handrailing can also be used as the bench backrest.

Benches can be constructed from many different materials, but they will look better if they are made from the same materials as used on the deck, stairs, and railings. If the spa has decorative tile inserts, you might consider integrating some of these tiles into the bench seats.

The seat portion of the bench will collect moisture from wet bathing suits, landscape watering, and from the evening dew, so there should be spaces between the seat boards to allow drainage. As with the railings, all bench surfaces must be smooth and splinter free because these surfaces will be used by people in bathing suits, and children may crawl on them.

Benches do not necessarily have to be built into the deck and railing system; they can be freestanding and portable. However, even freestanding benches should be made of the same materials as used for the deck, stairs, and railings.

Protection From Moisture

Like the benches, the deck surface will get wet from splashed spa water, rain, landscape watering, and dew. To maintain the deck wood, protect it from all types of moisture. If the wood used to build the deck surface was pressure treated with a preservative, it will not require as much protection as untreated wood. When a wood preservative is applied by soaking, brushing, or spraying, it must be reapplied at routine intervals, usually every two to three years, depending on the

quality of the preservative and on climatic conditions. Application intervals and directions are printed on the label. Some wood preservatives may even restore the original color to the wood if it has weathered.

If containers of plants and trees are placed on the deck, they must be kept off the surface by positioning spacers between the container and the deck. Spacers can be made of wood, brick, or plastic; they will allow air to circulate under the container and enable water to drain off or evaporate. If the container rests directly on the deck surface, the wood will remain wet and eventually will be damaged.

The well-chosen color of this spa blends with the colors of the deck and wooded surroundings.

Any spa location can be improved with a gazebo, shelter, or entertainment area. A gazebo can add beauty and privacy, a shelter can block wind or rain, and an entertainment area can make the spa a social center.

Gazebo, Shelter, and Entertainment Area

There is nothing like a relaxing soak in your spa—unless it's raining or the sun is just too hot to be comfortable. For situations like this, consider protecting the spa with a gazebo or an overhead shelter. This structure can be permanent, but if it is portable or adjustable, the area over the spa can be covered or open, depending on your mood or the weather conditions. Don't try to use trees or foliage for this purpose because the debris they generate will fall into the spa.

The roof structure can be made in different configurations to satisfy different requirements. It can be solid, transparent, opaque, or partially open with latticework or staggered boards. If you live in a cold climate you may want a solid but transparent roof made of plastic or tempered-glass panels that keep out the rain but let in the sun's warm rays. The roof can be built so it is partially open to allow filtered sunlight to shine through. This type of roof can be equipped with roll-up canvas panels or other materials that can completely close off the roof area to sunlight, if so desired.

The garden gazebo is very popular with spa owners and can easily become the focal point of the yard. You can build your own gazebo from scratch or purchase one of the prefabricated units that are available in many different shapes and sizes. Some gazebo manufacturers build the floor of their units to accept a standard-sized portable spa. Some spa manufacturers also offer custom-built gazebos that are designed to

A pavilion with a Victorian flavor draws the eye to this spa.

complement their specific spa. Some are quite elaborate; they may include steps, an eating area or bar with ornamental tile, decorative panels, stained glass, and awnings. Some also include lockable side panels and a door that can be locked to secure the spa completely.

Gazebos and shelters can be built from just about any type of material. You can use wood, steel, aluminum, or fiberglass, or any combination, to create an interesting structure that can be integrated nicely with either the spa or deck.

If the yard is large enough, you can repeat the same type of structure used with the spa elsewhere in the yard, and it can serve as the entertainment area separate from the spa. This area can be equipped with a built-in barbecue, a sink for food preparation, seating and tables, interior and exterior lighting, and even a music center. The other option is to build the spa into this entertainment area so everything is located in one place.

Spa Controls Enclosure

If the spa controls are not an integral part of the spa, they should be securely placed in a single lockable enclosure. Having all controls in one area is convenient, but the most important thing is that they are secured and can be operated only by the person or persons in charge of the spa. This helps to eliminate unauthorized use of the spa.

This custom spa-and-pool combination features a swim-up bar; just below the surface of the water are stools built into the bottom of the pool.

Top: Dramatic lighting brings out the beauty of this custom spa at night. Bottom: Daylight reveals the decking surface of nonslip slate imported from China.

PLANNING THE INDOOR SPA

Placing the spa indoors opens up a world of possibilities, from a quiet, soothing interlude in a master bedroom suite to social soaking in an entertainment room.

The indoor spa allows year-round use; driving rain can be part of the scenery, viewed through a picture window, instead of a reason to leave the spa.

This chapter will tell you how to plan an indoor spa: how to pick the room, how to prepare the house, and how to make the spa surroundings pleasant. The fourth chapter provides construction details.

The large windows of this indoor spa room allow an expansive water view; the skylight can be retracted, admitting ocean fragrances and the sound of breaking waves to enhance the visual experience.

AN INDOOR SPA?

The indoor spa allows complete freedom of use, never restricted by weather or time of day. It can be a luxurious accessory or the focal point of its own room.

Advance Planning

All spas, including swim spas (see page 48), can be installed outdoors or indoors, but if you live where the cold of the winter months is severe, you should consider an indoor spa. This will allow you to enjoy the warm spa without having to take a chilly walk through the backyard. Rain is a consideration any time of year. This is especially true if you live in an area that gets a lot of rain during the cold winter months. Installing the spa indoors also eliminates the need to add extra insulation to the spa and winterize the support equipment and plumbing.

If you and your family are involved in physical fitness, consider installing the spa, or perhaps a larger swim spa, indoors in an exercise room. If these activities suit your family's life-style, you can modify an existing room or add a room large enough to include the spa and exercise equipment.

Security is another reason to locate the spa indoors. Even in a safe and secure neighborhood, there is always the possibility of an uninvited person coming into your yard at night when you are using the spa.

Another consideration when planning an indoor spa is that any large body of warm water tends to cause humidity. The added moisture from the

spa can be a welcome relief if you live in a desert area or a very dry region, but it is not desirable if you live where the climate is normally humid, especially during the summer months. If the humidity is unwanted, it can be ventilated to the outdoors by a number of means described later in this chapter.

The best way to control humidity is also the easiest: keep the spa covered when it is not in use. The cover will contain the moist air and also keep any chemical odor to a minimum.

Try to eliminate the humidity from the room by natural air flow instead of using a fan or dehumidifier, which may be noisy. Covering the walls with untreated wood paneling will also help absorb moisture from the air. A detailed description of ventilation methods is provided later in this chapter.

If you are an indoor gardener, your plants should thrive in this warm humid room, since most indoor plants love moisture. Their foliage will add softness to the decor, and they will also help muffle some of the noise. Installing a spa in an existing room requires comprehensive preliminary planning. You must figure out

which room in the house is best suited for spa activity. You must also try to gauge what effect the spa room will have on the total use of the house. Will it be used just for the spa, or will it be an entertainment area for other types of activities? If your family is large and there are children, consider how the spa room will be used, by whom and when. Involve the whole family to avoid such a question from a child, "What do you mean I can't invite my friends over to use the spa when you're not at home?" Try to discuss all positive aspects as well as any potential problems that may arise so that everyone in the family will end up enjoying the new family toy.

The spa room should have a quiet, relaxing atmosphere when the spa is being used. Hot soaking is associated with relaxation, so locate the spa in a part of the house away from heavy traffic flow. This is especially true if there are small children in the house. Try to locate the spa room in a corner, or where there will be little or no cross traffic during spa time.

If the spa room does not have a shower or changing area, the spa should be located as close as possible to a bathroom, changing room, or shower room to reduce wet foot traffic through the house.

If there are children in the household, be sure to have lockable doors leading to the spa room. This way the room can be secured to prevent accidents, or the unsupervised use of the spa by your children and any of their friends.

Bringing the Spa Inside

When using an existing room in the house, you must plan how you are going to get the spa into the house and into its designated room. The new spa may be brought into the house through one of the exterior doors, through a room or series of rooms, or maybe even down a hallway before it reaches the new spa room. Will the spa assembly fit through the doorways, or will it have to pass through a large window? If you are unable to move the spa into the desired room, part of an exterior wall may have to be removed for access.

Even though a portable spa is designed to fit through an interior doorway when placed on its side, you will want to make sure that you can get it into the room you have chosen. If you have ever moved a large piece of furniture within your house, such as a king-sized mattress or box spring, you know how hard it is to move something that large through a hallway and into a room. The larger the spa, the harder it will be to move around within the house. In some cases, the size of the spa may be determined by how difficult it would be to move into the spa room.

If the spa is to be installed in a new room or addition, the problems are minimal. If the spa is too large to go through the doors or windows, it can be placed in the new room before the final framing.

Modifying the structure of your house to accept a spa requires detailed research and planning. The structure must be strong, plumbing and wiring must be added, and ventilation must be adequate for the humidity generated by the spa.

The Floor and Foundation

As you decide where to place the spa, consider the fact that it is very heavy and must be properly supported. If you have a two-story house, the top floor should be ruled out unless you are willing to go to a lot of expense to reinforce the floor area beneath the spa. The same is true if you want to place the spa above a basement. Although piers, posts, and girders could be used in the basement to provide support for the spa, the posts would obstruct the room and limit its usefulness.

If the spa is going to be placed on an existing floor, the floor—and possibly the foundation—must be redesigned and reinforced to support the additional weight of the spa once it is filled with water and people. The typical wood-framed floor and most concrete slab floors are designed and built to carry about 40 pounds of weight per square foot. In order to support the weight of the spa, you must calculate the spa weight per square foot that will be transferred to the floor surface. For example, if the spa weighs 8,500 pounds when filled with water and people and the bottom surface area of the spa is 35 square feet, divide the spa weight of 8,500 pounds by the 35-square-foot area of the spa. This equals approximately 243 pounds per square foot. Once the weight per square foot is established, consult your local building code or ask a qualified architect or builder to determine the flooring substructure that will be required to support the additional load.

If the spa is to be permanently installed within the floor and at floor level,

Preparing a Wood Floor for a Spa Installation

Cut away floor and support edges of hole

Concrete pad

Spa

Piers, posts, and girders

a concrete pad of the correct thickness can be poured in the ground to support the spa. If the new spa is a portable type and will be placed on the existing floor, the floor and foundation must be strengthened to support the additional weight of the filled spa. Usually, only the floor area directly below the spa is modified to carry the extra weight, so the location of the spa within the room must be decided before starting the construction. If the spa is to be installed in a newly added-on room, the floor for that room must be designed to support the spa. Again, the building code or an architect can help you determine this structural requirement.

Plumbing

The spa water system of most spas is a closed-loop design wherein the water moves from the spa to the support equipment for cleaning and heating and then back to the spa again. There is no freshwater inlet or dirty-water drain outlet built into the spa water system. Spas are usually drained and refilled with a garden hose. To fill the spa, the hose is connected to an existing hose bibb and the spa is filled with fresh cold water. To drain the spa, refer to the information in the fifth chapter (see pages 102 to 103). Spa water is chemically treated, and special considerations must by taken into account when draining it.

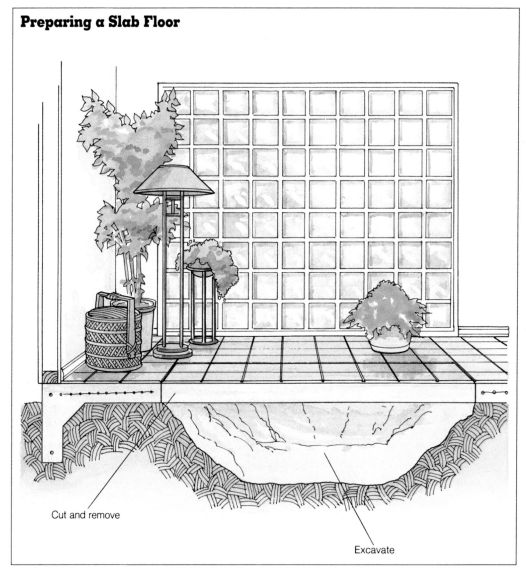

Preparing a Slab Floor

Cut and remove

Excavate

If the location of the spa within the house makes it difficult to fill or drain the water by using a hose from outside, you should consider adding a freshwater line with a hose bibb, and a drain line and fitting, in the spa room.

If the spa is heated with a fossil-fuel heater, a natural gas line or fuel oil line must be run from the main source in the house to the water heater for the spa; this procedure is covered in the fourth chapter (see pages 88 to 89). For an indoor spa, the fossil-fuel heater is usually placed outside the house because of the heat it generates; venting is also easier with exterior installation. Some fossil-fuel heaters can be installed indoors and vented to the outside.

Electricity

The electrical service for a 110-volt portable spa can usually be plugged into a dedicated circuit (one that is used only for the spa) with a 20-amp rating. A 220-volt portable spa must be permanently wired and usually requires a 50-amp dedicated circuit.

The electrical requirements for permanently installed spas vary because they have different types of electrical support

Spa Installed in a Slab Floor

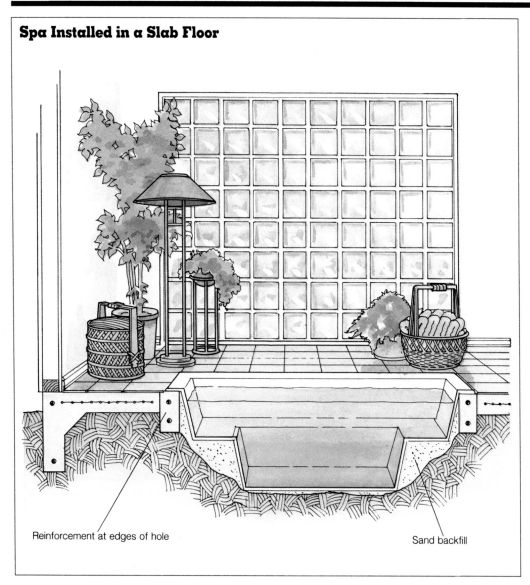

Reinforcement at edges of hole

Sand backfill

equipment. Usually this type of installation requires a dedicated circuit for each piece of electrical equipment. Most building electrical codes require the installation of ground fault circuit interrupter (GFCI) circuit breakers to protect any underwater spa lights and all electrical outlets within 15 feet of the spa. This type of circuit breaker shuts off the circuit almost

instantaneously to prevent accidental electric shocks in the case of any electrical difficulties relating to that circuit.

The additional circuit breakers for the spa must fit into the main service panel of the house. If the existing house main service panel is filled to capacity, an additional service panel must be installed to handle the added electrical requirements of the spa. If a new service panel is to

be added, install one large enough to accommodate not only the new spa requirements but also any future electrical needs. After the spa is installed and in use for a while, you may decide to add features to the spa or the spa room, and this may require an additional electrical circuit. Installing extra circuit

capacity now will save money in the future.

As discussed in the fourth chapter (see page 90), all electrical component installations should be handled by a licensed electrical contractor. If you plan to wire the spa yourself, seek the advice of a qualified electrician.

Ventilation

An indoor spa generates a lot of humidity that may or may not be desirable. This depends on what the normal humidity is in your geographic location. If the humidity is not wanted, then it must be removed from the room. This can be accomplished by adding adjustable skylights that can be opened to the outdoors, windows for cross-ventilation, sliding patio doors, exhaust vents, or a dehumidifier.

Cross-ventilation is the best way to clear the room of unwanted moisture. The natural breezes will travel through the room and take the humidity outside along with them. If the room is located on the corner of the house or extends out from the house, you can install large windows or sliding patio doors to achieve the maximum ventilation. If there is a prevailing breeze through the yard, try to locate the patio doors or windows to take advantage of this air flow.

If the roof structure of the spa room allows it, you can add several openable skylights that will allow the hot moist air that normally collects around the ceiling to dissipate naturally.

Movable Louvers

Along with the skylights, additional air flow can be generated by using a small fan to direct the humidity toward the open skylights.

If natural air flow will not provide sufficient circulation to remove the humidity, wall-mounted exhaust fans can be used to eliminate the unwanted moisture from the room. The fans must be mounted on an exterior wall and as close to the ceiling as possible, since this is where the hot moist air is trapped. The air-flow capacity of the exhaust fan or fans must be matched to the size of the room; it should be able to exchange the total air volume in the room about every 5 to 10 minutes.

If all else fails, you can use an electric dehumidifier. This is an expensive solution, since dehumidifiers are costly to purchase and use; they are also usually noisy in operation.

Protection Against Spills

No matter how careful you are getting into and out of the spa, some water will be splashed onto the floor. The floor surface, whether the spa is portable or permanently installed, should be made of a waterproof material such as concrete, ceramic tile, sheet vinyl, brick, or flagstone. If you choose vinyl flooring, always use sheet vinyl; do not use vinyl squares as the moisture will collect between the seams causing the squares to loosen and buckle. Never use self-adhesive squares; they will not stick to the floor for long in a wet environment. Wood similar to that used on decks (for example, heart redwood or cedar) can also be used indoors to surround the spa, but pressure-treated wood should not be used indoors, since its odor will linger. If you use wood for the flooring, you may want to use the same type of wood to panel one or more walls in the room. Untreated wood paneling will absorb moisture and help rid the room of unwanted humidity.

Choose a flooring surface that is not slippery when wet or when walked on with wet bare feet. Ideally, the surface should be left porous to absorb moisture. If you choose vinyl or smooth glazed ceramic tile, be especially cautious and choose a pattern or texture that will not be too slippery when wet. If you do cover the floor

The waterproof tile floor in this spa room solves the problem of damage from splashed water.

Moisture Protection for an Indoor Spa

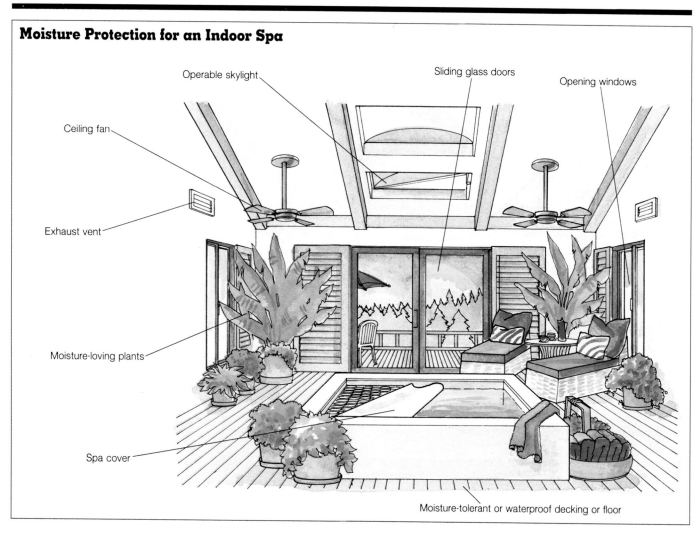

Operable skylight

Sliding glass doors

Opening windows

Ceiling fan

Exhaust vent

Moisture-loving plants

Spa cover

Moisture-tolerant or waterproof decking or floor

with either of these materials, consider placing a nonskid surface such as indoor/outdoor carpeting on the floor where people step out of the spa. This will lessen the possibility of accidents on a wet floor.

If the spa will be used mainly by the family in a controlled atmosphere, a flat floor surface with no drain angle is acceptable. Minimal amounts of spilled water can be wiped up or mopped up easily. If the spa will be used frequently and by a lot of people, the best solution is to install a floor with an angle that slopes to a drain outlet in the floor, which is then connected to the house drain line. This is the most expensive but also the most efficient way to divert a lot of spilled water. The floor drain can also be used when emptying the dirty water from the spa for cleaning.

Another reason to use a waterproof floor surface is to protect the floor structure beneath the spa. This is very important if the spa room has a wood-framed floor. If the floor structure below the spa becomes wet and stays wet, dry rot will set in, and the structure will be damaged and eventually will have to be replaced.

A waterproof dam or lip made of the same material as the flooring must be installed if the waterproof flooring surrounds just the spa, and the rest of the room is covered with carpeting or other nonwaterproof material. This dam will prevent the water from seeping under the nonwaterproof material and damaging it.

CHOOSING THE SPA LOCATION

Whether it's in a master bedroom retreat or the center of an entertainment room, the location of the spa will affect the way it is used. The spa will provide years of pleasure; think about how you will use it in the future as well as on the day it is installed.

Access and Privacy

What is the best all-around location for the spa in your house? If you envision using the spa for entertaining as well as family use, there must be easy access to the spa room. Don't locate the spa where the guests must walk through other rooms and down a hallway to get to it. The exception to this is the family room, which normally has a lot of foot traffic.

Ideally, the spa room should be located in a quiet area. When you are in the spa relaxing after a day at work, you will probably want peace and quiet. So you can soak in serenity, the spa room should be located in the quietest section of the house and also away from any outside noise, such as street activity, a loud neighbor, or barking dogs.

The indoor spa allows hot soaking in complete privacy. The spa room should be designed to be closed off to walk-through traffic. For maximum privacy the room can be enclosed by screens or blinds to block off all exposure from the outside. If there are small children in the family, you must be able to lock the spa room to prevent accidents, or to keep the older children and their friends from using the spa when you are not at home.

A dramatic sloped ceiling, opened by a skylight, sets off this master bedroom spa, which has a shower and changing room just a few steps away (opposite page).

After the indoor spa is installed and the interior decor is completed, the entire room can be a real showplace; it can also become the center for family activities. If you do a lot of entertaining that includes dining and barbecuing, the indoor spa can be a focal point.

If the spa room is not close to the kitchen, you may want to consider adding a food preparation area, with a wet bar and a small refrigerator for snacks and soft drinks. This will make entertaining easier and it will also be handy for family activities.

Existing Rooms

The location of the spa within the house should be determined by how the spa will be used most of the time. Is the spa just for your own use, or will it also be used by your guests? If the spa is strictly for personal use, a very desirable location is the master bathroom or master bedroom.

Master Bedroom or Bathroom

Either of these locations is ideal for an intimate relaxing time away from the rest of the family. With the spa located in either of these places, it is very easy to take a shower, have a hot soak, dry off, and then get into bed without having to get dressed to go from room to room. If you are planning to have guests use the spa, these locations are not recommended, however, since most people, even good friends, will probably be uncomfortable using a spa in someone else's bedroom or bathroom. Give these locations considerable thought, since they do restrict the spa to personal use. After you realize how much you enjoy the spa yourself, you might wish it were located elsewhere so your friends could join you for this type of relaxation.

Garage

If you are really cramped for space in the house and there is no spare room for a spa, consider converting the garage into a spa room. Many garages, especially attached garages, have been converted into family rooms; why not use one for a spa room? If you decide on this location, check the local building code to see if it is legal. Large windows can be added and skylights can be installed to let humidity evaporate and add brightness to the room. The walls and ceiling can be insulated with a vapor barrier to repel the moisture; you can then install paneling or wallboard.

Once the floor is refinished and some special lighting and comfortable furniture are added, that dusty old garage can be transformed into a very livable indoor room with a spa.

One other area to consider is the garage roof, if the garage is attached to a two-story house and the garage roof extends out from the house. The garage roof structure can be removed and a new floor constructed in its place as the base for a new spa room. The entrance to the new spa room can be from a second-story room or hallway or via an outside staircase. The new room can be built like a standard addition or like a greenhouse room. If the garage is large enough, you can also add a small deck.

The Add-On Spa Room

If there is no room in the house, and the garage is out of the question, a completely new spa room can be added to the house. This can be a custom-built room using standard house-construction methods, or it can be a prefabricated unit. With proper planning, a custom-built room can be integrated into the overall design of the existing house; it doesn't need to look like an addition. In building a customized addition, you can include all the features you think will make the spa room enjoyable. Your available budget is the only limiting factor for the choice of features to be included. If possible, visit friends who have an interior spa room and find out what they like and don't like about the layout. Consider what their life-style is like and whether you plan to use your spa room the same way that they use theirs.

If a custom-built room is not feasible, the spa room can be a prefabricated enclosure attached to the exterior of the house. These types of room enclosures may or may not fit with the architecture of your

This corner sunroom gives an outdoor feeling to an indoor spa.

house. Some house designs will blend well with this type of room enclosure, whereas others will not. Be cautious, because you don't want a structure that looks like an afterthought. If you are considering this type of addition, look at some completed rooms and see if you are happy with the end results. How well are they integrated into the house?

Add-on room enclosures can be purchased in prefabricated kits from home-improvement centers and at remodeling and home-improvement shows. These kits vary in price and range from bare-bones layouts to elaborate structures. Most prefabricated kits consist of an aluminum, steel, or wooden frame with glass or plastic side panels and solid roof panels. The glass panels can be of either single- or double-glazed construction. They include roof panels, which usually have a low-emissivity solar finish to reflect the sun and reduce heat buildup within the room. These rooms also often have movable panels to close off the view from the outside or to block direct sunlight.

Add-on rooms are usually placed on a concrete slab poured for the purpose. If you choose this method, be sure to let the contractor know you plan to place a spa on the slab.

If there is a deck attached to the house, it could become the basis for a new spa room. The deck could be reinforced to accept the additional weight of the spa and enclosed with a room enclosure system similar to that used for a modular greenhouse.

This lushly landscaped spa room is at the center of the house; the other rooms open onto it.

An indoor spa provides unique decorating opportunities and challenges. Well-planned decor can combine the advantages of an entertainment center and a private bathing nook. A convenient shower and changing room can prevent traffic problems.

Shower and Changing Room

If you have enough space in the house, consider building a shower and changing room for your guests either within the spa room or as close to it as possible.

This room has the same advantages, and should have the same features, as the shower and changing rooms described in the first chapter (see page 17).

Entertainment Area

If the spa room is large enough, it can be the center of family activity and also can be used for entertaining. The room can be designed so the spa is either the center of interest or a pleasant component, depending on the type of entertaining you do.

The room can include the spa or swim spa and any number of other features, such as an area for exercise equipment, a shower and changing room, wet bar, food preparation and eating areas, pool table, furniture for lounging and relaxation, or a music and television center. If the room is designed correctly, you can throw a party in it, and none of the other rooms in the house will be needed.

However, if the spa is located in a room of such size, you may not have as quiet an atmosphere as you want. To have the best of both worlds, you can locate the spa in one corner of the room and use a portable divider to close off the spa area for private soaking.

Decor

You can furnish the room in any motif you desire. Just because the spa is filled with water doesn't mean that the room has to look like a tropical island. In fact, you may want to carry the decorating theme of the rest of your house into the spa room. The room can be very elegant, with stained-glass or beveled-glass windows, or very casual, depending on your decorating preference.

Choose the furniture, fabrics, colors, wall coverings, and flooring so they will harmonize with the spa. All of the furniture and other components within the spa room must work well together as an

Sample Floor Plans for Indoor Spas

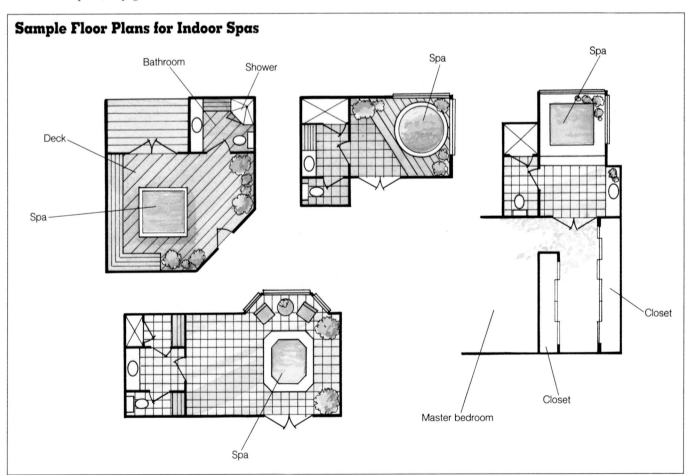

integrated design to create a room that is enjoyable and attractive.

When choosing the furniture and fabrics, remember that the room will be humid. Be sure to take this into consideration if you are going to install drapes. Avoid a heavy drapery material that will absorb moisture, because this can eventually lead to mildew and damage to the material. Choose a fabric that is lightweight and one that will resist moisture. If you are going to place any furniture adjacent to the spa, make sure it is water-resistant, preferably a high-quality grade of plastic patio furniture. People will be coming out of the spa with bathing suits that are wet and that may contain chemicals. If chlorine is used in the spa water, it will bleach any fabric that it touches. So choose your furniture carefully to avoid possible damage to any fabric-covered surfaces.

Some artwork can also be damaged by humidity. Check with experts before placing art objects in the spa room.

Try to integrate plants into the decor. They will add softness to the room. The plants can hang from wall brackets or from the ceiling, or they can be placed on the floor in large decorative pots. If the room is large, you can even place small trees in attractive containers. Choose plants and trees that thrive in humidity; they should prosper in this environment.

A wall-mounted television and glass-block bar surround this spa with entertainment possibilities. The bar includes built-in lights.

S ELECTING THE SPA

Choosing the correct spa can be quite a complicated process. There are a number of different spa configurations and many types of support equipment. Some people want the spa for hydrotherapy purposes, whereas others plan to use it just for relaxation. This chapter will guide you through all the decisions required to find a spa you will be happy with when you sit down for your first relaxing hot soak.

Home-improvement and remodeling shows are a good place to start your search for a spa. The home sections of local newspapers often advertise these events. The shows bring together many of the major spa manufacturers, dealers, and service organizations in your immediate area.

In many cases spa dealers will offer special show prices on spas and equipment. These specials may offer substantial savings, but you should do some comparison shopping before attending the shows to be sure you're getting a good buy.

Buying a spa can be a major financial investment, so be sure to do your research. Don't rush into buying something simply because it seems to be a good buy; this could result in money poorly spent. If you know exactly what you're looking for and research the available options thoroughly, you will be able to find a spa package that meets your needs.

Spa showrooms provide the opportunity to inspect several spas at once; you can also find answers to your questions and give the spas the all-important soak test.

TYPES AND SIZES OF SPAS

Once you have selected the location, it's time to select the spa. Whether you're looking for a built-in or portable spa, a casual or formal arrangement, the market offers a wealth of choices. You should look at many models before you decide.

Luxury Bathtub, Hot Tub, or Spa

Luxury bathtubs and spas are very similar in design and function. The main difference is that luxury tubs are filled with fresh water for each use then drained afterward. Spas have a heating and filtration system that allows the water to be reused.

Hot tubs resemble barrels and are always made of wood.

Permanent Spa or Portable Spa?

The choice between a built-in or portable spa depends mainly on how much money you want to invest, what your specific needs are, and how long you plan to stay in your current residence. If you are renting a house, or your career requires frequent moves, you should consider a portable spa, which can be packed up along with the rest of your furnishings.

Built-in spas are manufactured from a variety of materials and can take on almost any shape, size, and depth. Built-in spas cost more to install since they are partially or completely sunk into the ground or floor.

A permanent outdoor spa requires excavation of the yard for spa placement, and installation of the support equipment, plumbing, and electrical components. A permanent indoor spa requires modification of an existing floor or room, which is costly. The support equipment for a built-in spa is usually placed at a distance from the spa, resulting in quieter surroundings. Since this type of spa is more expensive and more permanent, its location should be thoroughly planned, as detailed in the first chapter for outdoor spas (page 10), or the second chapter for indoor spas (page 38).

The portable spa is constructed so it can fit through an interior doorway, enabling it to be placed either indoors or outdoors. It can even be moved back and forth for year-round use if you live in a climate with extreme temperature changes between summer and winter. The one big advantage of a portable spa is that it can be purchased, delivered, installed, and put to use in a very short period of time. The sides of the portable spa are covered with a skirting, usually of redwood or other decorative material. In order to integrate the spa into an outdoor environment, a gazebo, raised deck, or entertainment area can be added.

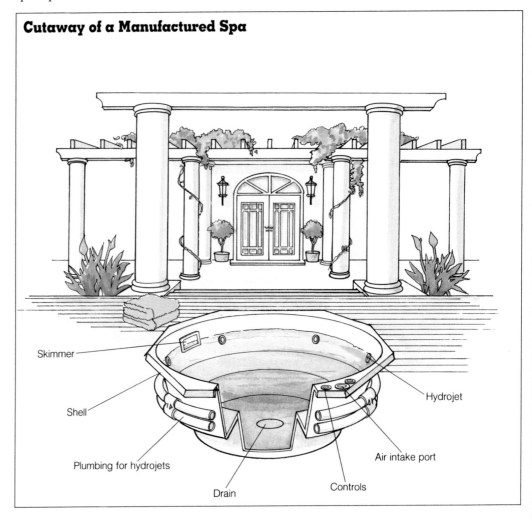

Cutaway of a Manufactured Spa

Skimmer

Shell

Plumbing for hydrojets

Drain

Controls

Hydrojet

Air intake port

Cutaway of a Custom-built Spa

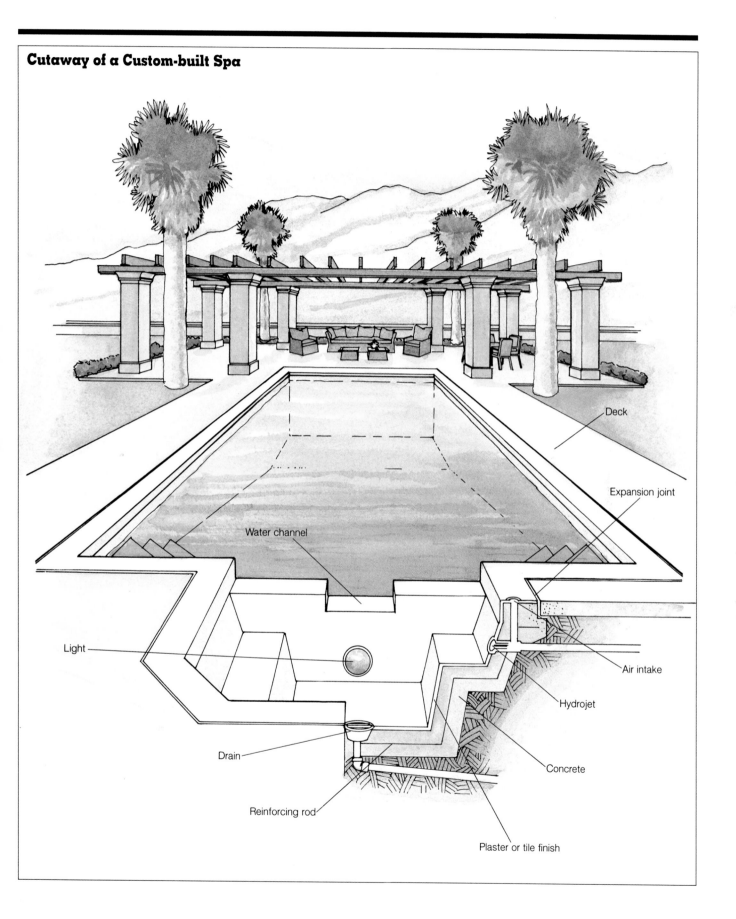

Deck

Expansion joint

Water channel

Light

Air intake

Hydrojet

Drain

Concrete

Reinforcing rod

Plaster or tile finish

In many areas, there is no need to procure a building permit to install a portable spa, but it does have to be installed according to local building codes, especially the electrical code. The electrical outlet for the support equipment must be protected by a ground fault circuit interrupter (GFCI) for safety reasons. Be sure to check your local building code to see whether a permit is required, since different communities have different building codes.

Size of the Spa

The size of the spa depends on your specific needs. Is your family large? Do you entertain a lot and have a large number of guests? Do you want to just relax and soak or do you want to exercise and swim?

For soaking, the spa need not be large and can be either built-in or portable. There are many designs available for those who want a spa for relaxing and soaking, and you should be able to find one with just the shape, size, and features you desire.

Swim Spas

The swim spa can be installed as a built-in or aboveground unit, either indoors or outdoors. If you want to use the spa for exercising and swimming, and your yard is not large enough for a swimming pool, the swim spa may suit your needs perfectly. This type of spa is usually rectangular and, although it is not long enough to swim laps, it allows you to exercise by swimming in place against a current created by the hydrojets of the

Cutaway of a Portable Spa

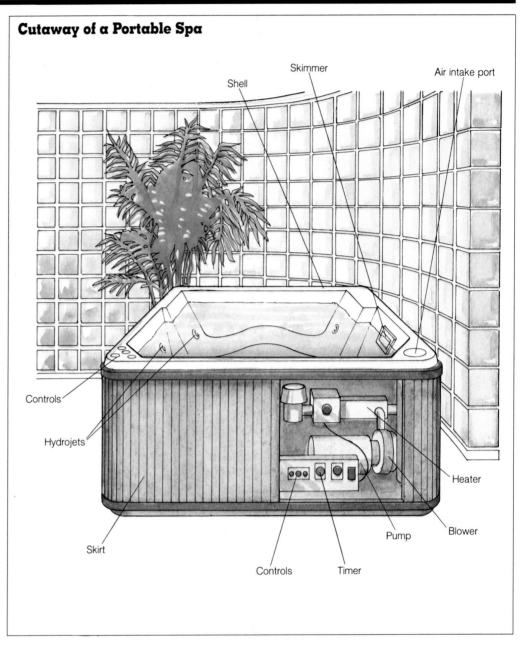

spa. The swim spa is equipped with multiple high-output pumps connected to swim hydrojets located at one end of the spa. The pumps and hydrojets can create a current of about 3 to 4 miles per hour to swim against; the force of

the current is adjustable. On some models, air can also be introduced into the swim hydrojets to increase the power of the current. Be sure to test a swim spa before you buy it. The range of current adjustment on some swim spas may not suit your needs.

Some swim spas also incorporate a soaking spa at one end. This type of spa has a dual-control temperature feature,

which allows for higher water temperature in the soaking part of the spa and cooler water temperature in the swimming portion. Dual-purpose spas of this type allow you to take a relaxing hot soak after a vigorous swimming workout.

Manufactured spas are available
with tile surfaces for a custom look.

Shade cloth, which offers varying
degrees of protection from sunlight,
is a simple, attractive way to shelter
a spa.

The dark-tile lane indicator in this spa, which matches those in racing pools, is a familiar touch for lap swimmers.

Spas and Swimming Pools

Are you planning to add a swimming pool and a spa? If these are installed at the same time, both units can be integrated into one design and can share the same support equipment, saving a lot of money.

If you purchased a house with an existing swimming pool, a spa can be added at any time. Depending on the size and type of the spa, it may be possible to link the new spa equipment to the swimming pool support equipment.

Complementary colors and materials provide a pleasing visual integration of this spa and swimming pool.

Wooden Hot Tubs

The hot tub is a watertight round or oval vat made of various types of rot-resistant wood. A hot tub is similar to a barrel used to age wine or whiskey. In fact, some of the early hot tubs were modified half-barrels discarded by wineries or distillers.

The wooden hot tub has historical roots in Europe and Asia. This ancient history includes the Japanese *furo*, which uses very hot water and is large enough for only one person sitting upright.

The hot tub is constructed using the age-old coopering method of barrel-making. Barrels and hot tubs are made by using beveled wooden slats, or staves, a flat floor, and metal bands to hold the slats and floor together. The wood used in constructing a hot tub is usually heartwood that is free of knots and sapwood. The most popular woods are redwood, cedar, and mahogany.

Wooden hot tubs have a warm, natural appearance that complements the natural wooded landscape of a backyard.

The wooden hot tub has advantages and disadvantages. On the plus side, there is the feeling of soft warmth that a person experiences while soaking in a wooden hot tub. The wood feels more natural and friendlier against your body than do the slick, hard surfaces of the synthetic materials used in manufactured spas.

Even though the wooden hot tub can be made only in a round or oval shape, it can be deeper than most spas. This extra depth allows complete body immersion all the way up to your neck.

On the minus side, the wooden hot tub requires strict routine maintenance to keep both the water and wood in proper condition. If the maintenance program is neglected, the wood will be damaged and may not be repairable. Water chemistry must be maintained perfectly to eliminate the possibility of bacterial growth or decay of the wood. In severe cases bacteria can enter into the wood pores and spread infection to anyone who uses the tub. The wooden hot tub must also be drained and cleaned more frequently than spas made from other materials. Also, it cannot be drained and left dry for any length of time because the wooden staves will shrink away from each other, forming permanent gaps between them.

The popularity of this kind of tub peaked in the early 1970s and has continued to decline, so that wooden hot tubs now represent only 1 percent of sales in the current spa and hot tub market.

HOW SPAS ARE BUILT

Spa construction techniques range from high-tech vacuum forming to hand-laid tile. The type of construction you choose will depend on your individual needs and preferences. This section will tell you what is available.

Permanent Spas— Indoors or Outdoors

The permanently installed spa shell can be made of vacuum-molded acrylic or plastic, or it can be made of more traditional materials, such as gunite, poured concrete, and tile.

The support equipment for a permanent spa is usually located some distance from the spa, which helps to create a quieter, more relaxing atmosphere than in portable spas, which have their support equipment integrated into the framework of the spa.

Shotcrete and Gunite

The permanent spa made of shotcrete or gunite is made just like a swimming pool and is used mainly in outdoor locations. This type of construction allows the creation of a soft free-form shape, unlike poured concrete-and-tile construction which is limited to flat planes.

Once the spa location is selected, the site is excavated in the basic shape of the spa. During the excavation the shape can even be changed slightly, provided the contractor will go along with the changes. When the excavation is done, the rough plumbing pipes, fittings, electrical fixtures, and conduit for lighting and support equipment are installed.

Then steel reinforcing bars, or rebars, are placed into the sides and base of the hole for strength, following the basic contour. The rebars are tied together where they intersect to form a framework. The shotcrete or gunite is applied uniformly over the framework with high-pressure hoses. The framework is completely filled to a uniform thickness, and all the rebars are covered. The shotcrete or gunite is then hand-troweled and smoothed out. After the shotcrete or gunite has dried, a special plaster precoat and final topcoat are applied to achieve a smooth surface. Usually, rows of decorative tiles are applied around the waterline to make spa upkeep easier. This also adds a nice finishing touch. After this phase is completed, the water, drain, and electrical hookups are connected.

This type of spa does have several disadvantages. The interior surface is rougher than other types of spas discussed in this chapter. The finished coat still has a slightly coarse surface, which tends to attract algae in the same way a swimming pool does. This type of spa must be cleaned more often to keep the algae under control.

Also, the chemicals within the final plaster coat will leach out into the first fill of water making it difficult to maintain the correct chemistry at first. After the plaster has cured

Rovel® thermoplastic, used for the shell of this spa, provides durability and attractiveness.

and the leaching has subsided, it will be easier to maintain the correct water chemistry.

Concrete and Tile

A concrete-and-tile spa can be very beautiful and may even resemble a large Roman bath. It is best suited to an outdoor spa but could be used indoors as well. This is the most expensive type of spa construction and is not common in today's market. It is used primarily in areas where shotcrete and gunite are not readily available. The spa design always uses flat sides and bottom, which can be built using rigid wooden forms.

As with gunite spas, the location is selected and excavated. Wooden forms that conform to the shape of the spa are then built on the site. Steel reinforcing bars are placed into the

forms for strength and tied together where they intersect. At this time the rough plumbing pipes and fittings, electrical fixtures, and conduit for lighting and support equipment are installed. The forms are then completely filled with concrete, usually supplied by a transit-mix concrete company.

After the concrete has cured, the forms are removed and the water, drain, and electrical hookups are connected. The area outside the spa is then backfilled with dirt or sand, if necessary. The interior surface is smoothed out as much as possible. Ceramic tile may then be applied to all interior surfaces. An alternative approach is to apply a special plaster precoat and final topcoat, as with a gunite spa, and finish off with rows of decorative tiles around the waterline.

Tile Backing Board With Tile, Marble, Granite, or Onyx

Some spas are prefabricated using tile backing board and tile, marble, granite, or onyx. Spas manufactured using this method resemble concrete-and-tile spas but have some important advantages. Although this type of spa looks expensive, it is competitive in price with acrylic or plastic molded spas. This type of construction lends itself to both indoor and outdoor installations.

Many standard spa and swim spa designs are available in this style, and custom-built spas can be fabricated with a very short lead time. This type of spa is manufactured at a factory and the finished product, which is lightweight, is trucked to the job site ready for installation.

The spa is manufactured over a plywood male mold. If the spa will have a finished veneer of ceramic tile, the surfaces can be slightly curved, in one direction only. If marble, granite, or onyx will be used for the final course, all surfaces must be flat, since these pieces of material are usually larger than ceramic tile and are not curved.

Precut pieces of ⅜-inch-thick tile backing board with a vinyl-coated woven glass fiber mesh are placed onto the mold and held in place with special tape. This is called the intermediate layer. After the tile backing board is in place, it is covered completely with a ⅜-inch layer of reinforced fiberglass. Integral laminated supports are added to all seating and step areas and to any long spans (usually found in swim spas). The fiberglass bonds the backing board and supports together to form an integral outer spa shell.

At this time a strong, self-supporting wooden base is bonded to the exterior of the outer shell and is covered with fiberglass to make it impervious to moisture. After the fiberglass has cured, the spa shell and wooden support base unit are removed from the mold. Holes are cut in the outer spa shell for the drain, hydrojets, lighting fixtures, and other equipment.

The interior surface material (tile, marble, granite, or onyx) is then applied to the inner surface of the tile backing board with an epoxy-based grout, creating the finished surface. The cement backing board is designed specifically for use with tile and grout and therefore forms a long-lasting bond with the tile or other material. The grout lines are filled with the same epoxy-based grout. When the grout has cured, the unit is ready for installation of the plumbing and electrical components.

After these components are connected, the spa is filled with water for a leak test. After testing, the unit is ready for shipping and installation.

Fiberglass and Gelcoat

This type of construction was considered a breakthrough many years ago and offered the first smooth-surfaced spa that could be fabricated in almost any shape and size. The spa shell is made in a factory, then moved to the job site and installed. But the combination of fiberglass and gelcoat is no longer commonly used in manufacturing spas (it constitutes less than 2 percent of today's spa market). Problems with these materials were discovered after the spas had been in use for several years.

The gelcoat surface is a polyester resin with an added coloring agent. The surface is dull, requires a lot of maintenance, and will fade from exposure to sunlight. Also, the chemicals used daily in the spa water affect the surface appearance, which means it must be polished and reconditioned every few months.

This type of spa must be covered when not in use to reduce fading and damage. In some climates, the spa will have to be resurfaced about every four to five years. The more sun exposure, the sooner the spa will have to be resurfaced.

Another persistent problem is that the gelcoat surface will blister and even delaminate from the fiberglass backing. This causes water leaks, resulting in costly repairs.

Fiberglass-and-gelcoat spas should not be considered. It is no longer a state-of-the-art method of manufacturing a spa, especially when compared with the more durable methods and materials of today.

Acrylic

The acrylic spa is just about ideal. The surface is nonporous, slick, shiny, and durable. The colors range from bright or subtle solids to a simulated marble finish in a variety of shades. Since the color permeates the acrylic sheet it lasts a long time if the spa is well maintained. Sunlight causes the acrylic surface to fade

This spa consists of an outer fiberglass shell, a core of concrete tile backing board, and a finish layer of tile, capped with brick. This type of construction allows a custom-built look in a manufactured spa.

slightly, so the spa should be covered when not in use.

The surface is not very susceptible to scratches, and any damage can be repaired with a special touch-up kit available from the spa manufacturer. Since different manufacturers may use slightly different types or grades of acrylic sheets, be sure to get a touch-up kit from the same company that made the spa shell.

The spa is formed from a single acrylic sheet, which is heated until pliable and then vacuum molded, or drawn, into a female mold. Once the formed acrylic sheet has cooled, it is removed from the mold.

By this time, the acrylic sheet has taken on the shape of the spa shell. The air channels and support-equipment fittings are then added to the shell. On some large spas, strengthening ribs are added at critical points, such as the seating areas and the base. Once these pieces are attached to the spa shell, fiberglass is applied to the backside for rigidity. The method of applying the fiberglass varies with different manufacturers, but the end result is the same—added strength for a longer-lasting spa.

Some manufacturers add a self-supporting wooden base to the spa shell at this time. This base is made of wood strong enough to support the spa and is then covered with fiberglass to make it impervious to moisture. The base makes the spa easier to install and level at the job site.

Spas can be made from a variety of materials. The appearance, and how well the material will blend with the surroundings you have chosen, should be considered along with its other characteristics.

Since the acrylic shell with its fiberglass backing is relatively thin, it has no insulating properties. Most spa manufacturers spray a thick coat of polyurethane foam insulation onto the entire backside. The foam provides good thermal insulation and also gives the spa a little more rigidity.

Once the insulating foam has cured, the hydrojets, air jets, and any lighting fixtures are installed. The plumbing for the water and drains is then attached, and the spa is ready to install.

This type of construction can be used for either a permanent or portable spa.

Rovel® Thermoplastic

Rovel® is a trade name for a high-impact weather-resistant thermoplastic material that is used in spa construction. This material has been used for years in the manufacture of pleasure-boat hulls, camper shells, and other recreational products previously made of fiberglass. Rovel® thermoplastic was developed for products that are exposed to harsh sunlight, temperature extremes, and possible impact damage. Under these circumstances this material will hold up better than acrylic or fiberglass.

Rovel® thermoplastic was first used in the early 1980s. It is currently used for about 10 to 15 percent of the spas manufactured in the United States; it is used as a layer over a base of ABS plastic, which is another high-strength, resilient thermoplastic. ABS has been used for years in plastic plumbing fittings and pipe for residential and recreational vehicles. Rovel® thermoplastic is thicker and stronger than acrylic and usually comes with a longer service warranty. It has all the features that acrylic has—a variety of colors, surface and color durability, and ease of cleaning and maintenance.

The best feature of Rovel® thermoplastic is that it is stronger than acrylic and does not have to be strengthened with a fiberglass backing. Rovel® spas are vacuum molded using the same manufacturing techniques as are used on acrylic spas. As with acrylic ones, Rovel® spas require an application of polyurethane foam to the backside for proper thermal insulation.

Rovel® thermoplastic can be used for either a permanent or portable spa.

Portable Aboveground Spas

The portable spa is constructed as a one-piece, self-contained unit. Most portable spas produced today have a spa shell made of vacuum-molded acrylic or Rovel® thermoplastic. The portable spa shell is manufactured in exactly the same way as if it were to be installed as a permanent unit, but it is housed in a wooden framework.

Once the spa shell is formed and plumbed, it is installed in a boxlike framework, which houses the spa shell and all of the support equipment. The support equipment is connected to the shell fittings and then installed into the support-equipment compartment in the framework. The framework is then covered by a perimeter skirt, which is usually made of clear, all-heart redwood or other decorative materials.

Industry-Accepted Brand-Name Spas and Support Equipment

Buying a spa is a major investment, so it must be thoroughly investigated prior to purchase. Whenever you buy a major household appliance, you want to know if it meets industry approval requirements. The same holds true when purchasing a spa.

National Spa and Pool Institute

The National Spa and Pool Institute (NSPI) is the governing body for the spa and pool industry. It sets manufacturing standards for spa builders and dealer organizations. The manufacturers and dealers who belong to this organization agree to abide by its standards.

NSPI guidelines specify the materials to be used in spa construction. The materials must be nontoxic to the user and must be unaffected by substances used to maintain safe water chemistry. The guidelines also regulate the structural design of the spa, the internal and external dimensions, spa-shell attachment and installation, support equipment, and safety factors.

The guidelines are continually updated to meet the needs of consumers and to respond to changes in the industry.

NSPI members agree to follow federal, state, and local regulations if these exceed NSPI guidelines.

Look for the NSPI logo on the manufacturer's, retailer's, or service company's publications and equipment.

Underwriters' Laboratory

The electric pump, air blowers, lighting, and all electrical equipment should bear the Underwriters' Laboratory (UL) seal. This means the component has been manufactured and tested in accordance with UL codes. Portable spas are approved as an entire assembly and must pass UL code 1563, Electric Hot Tubs, Spas, and Associated Equipment. If the component has the UL seal on it, it has passed the specified tests and is safe for use.

Make sure all electrical equipment has the UL seal of approval. All spa-related electrical components are used in a wet environment; when water and electricity are used in close proximity, there is always the danger of electric shocks.

American Gas Association

The gas water heater should bear the American Gas Association (AGA) seal. This seal means the heater has passed the AGA tests for spa or swimming pool use and can be used safely to heat spa water.

International Association of Plumbing and Mechanical Officials

The International Association of Plumbing and Mechanical Officials (IAPMO) is the governing body that regulates and tests plumbing components and fixtures sold in the United States for residential, industrial, and recreational vehicle plumbing.

Some of the better portable spas are totally insulated, which means that all the voids between the spa shell and the skirt are filled with a high-density polyurethane foam. This provides increased insulation and also helps to keep moisture from entering the underside of the unit. Other portable spas are insulated with rigid commercial insulation applied to the skirt.

Servicing a spa that is completely covered with foam insulation is difficult and time-consuming. Before the spa can be serviced, the foam insulation must be chiseled out in order to gain access to a faulty part or a leaking water pipe. After the servicing is finished, the insulation must be reapplied with a foam gun.

Optional Equipment for Portable Spas

When you purchase a portable spa, it is usually sold as a complete package—spa, support equipment, and skirting. The standard package of support equipment is designed to be compatible with the spa size and water volume within it. Some spa manufacturers offer optional equipment for their portable spas. These include covers, timers, and higher BTU-rated water heaters.

Energy Conservation

One of the most important considerations in spa construction is energy conservation. Attention to conserving energy starts when the spa shell is manufactured and follows throughout the installation. After the shell is formed, a layer of fiberglass is applied to some models. Then a thick layer of polyurethane foam thermal insulation is sprayed over the complete underside of the spa shell. The quality of the foam insulation depends on its density and thickness. Foam with high quality insulating properties (R-rating) should have a high density, equal to about 2 pounds per square foot. The better the spa is insulated, the longer the water will retain its heat.

Information such as the R-rating and thickness of the spa insulation is sometimes difficult to obtain from spa manufacturers and is usually not listed in the sales literature. If heat loss is an important concern in your area, the availability of this information should be a factor in deciding which brand of spa to buy. Spas tend to lose most of their water heat from the surface, with the remainder escaping through the sidewall. An insulated spa cover is the best way to reduce surface heat loss. These covers are discussed later in this chapter.

Water also loses heat through the hot-water pipes between the spa and the support equipment; much of this can be prevented by insulating the pipes and fittings. This procedure is covered in the fourth chapter (page 88).

PA EQUIPMENT

Equipment selection involves more than the obvious considerations of cost and quality. A large array of equipment is designed for a wide variety of situations. The arrangement and number of fittings can vary considerably, and these differences will affect the operation of the spa.

Skid Pack or Individual Components

A skid pack is a set of support-equipment components that is matched, hydraulically and electrically, to the needs of a specific type and size of spa. Most portable spas are equipped with a skid pack, and in most cases it is designed to be the one best suited to that particular unit. When choosing a portable spa, make sure the skid pack, which is located under the skirt, is equipped with quality components. Some spa manufacturers will let you choose different brands, while others will not.

The skid pack is sometimes slightly more expensive than individual components purchased separately, but it eliminates the possibility of mismatched parts because the skid pack is a complete unit that has been assembled and tested at the factory. This helps to alleviate problems when the assembly is connected to the spa on the job site.

The skid pack generally contains a water pump or pumps, filter, air blower, electric heater, control panel, timer, and valving. Usually there are two water lines from the skid pack that are connected to the spa

during installation. One water line is the suction line, which draws the cooler water from the spa, and the other is the return line, which discharges the filtered and heated water back into the spa. If the skid pack is equipped with an air blower, there will be an additional line going to the air bubbler on the spa.

Individual support-equipment components can be purchased for larger spas and swim spas; the dealer can help you determine the correct sizes for your spa. You should rely on the dealer's expertise for size

recommendations. Individual components give you the flexibility of changing to a larger unit. After the spa has been in use for a while, for instance, you may want a higher capacity heater or air blower.

Water Pump

The purpose of the water pump is to circulate water within the spa. The water is drawn from the spa through the suction line, filtered, heated, and then returned to the spa. Fresh water is not routinely added; the existing water

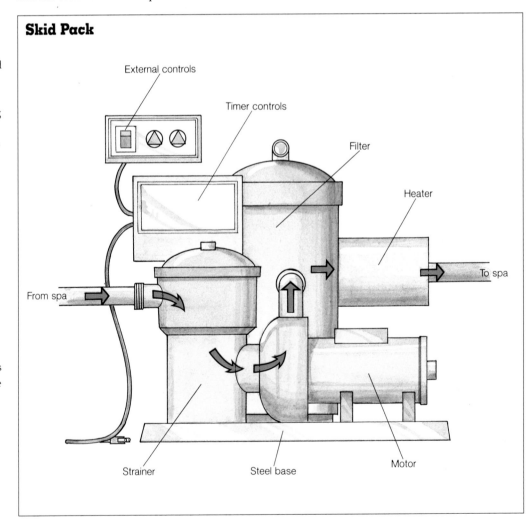

Skid Pack

External controls

Timer controls

Filter

Heater

From spa

To spa

Strainer

Steel base

Motor

is simply cleaned and recirculated. Fresh water is added to the spa only to replace water that has splashed out, or to refill the spa after draining and cleaning.

The size of the pump depends on the size of the spa, the number and type of hydrojets used, the size of the water pipes, and how freely the water can flow through the plumbing. One other consideration is the location of the support equipment in relation to the spa. If the pump has to move the water a long distance and through a series of plumbing elbows and fittings, the pump will have to be more powerful. If in doubt, purchase a pump that is a little more powerful than specified—but not a lot more powerful. If the pump is too forceful, it can damage the filter. If the pump is not strong enough, the water will not be kept crystal clear and the hydrojets will be unable to provide sufficient whirlpool action. Generally each hydrojet requires ¼ horsepower of pump power to function properly.

Water pumps are available in different power ratings ranging from ⅙ hp to 2 hp and can be designed to operate at 110 volts or 220 volts. Energy-efficient two-speed pumps are frequently used. The lower speed is used to circulate the water through the filter and heater; the higher speed is used for the hydrojets.

Large spas and swim spas usually require two separate pumps to operate efficiently. One pump generates water circulation and the other powers the hydrojets.

Water Pump

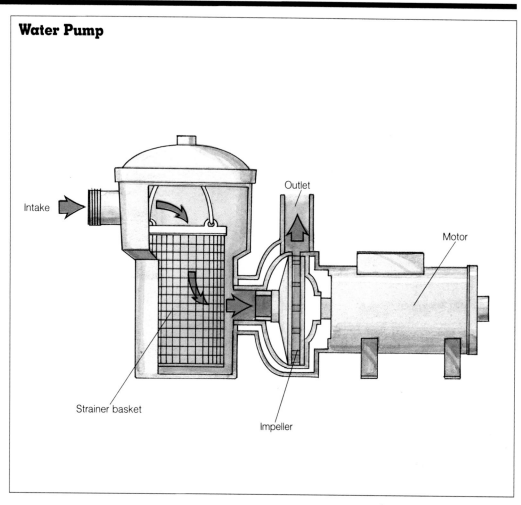

Spa water-pump impellers are normally made of plastic. In more expensive pumps, they are usually constructed of very durable Noryl® plastic. As the water enters the rotating pump impeller, it hits the center of the impeller and is thrown out toward the outer edge of the impeller by the vanes, thus creating the pumping action. On some pumps, a diffuser is used along with the impeller to create a better pumping action.

The diffuser is a round, flat plate that faces the impeller and has radiating fins or lines on it. The diffuser plate can get clogged over a period of time or can be gouged by small particles that pass through the filter. On some pumps, the diffuser plate can be replaced.

One critical part of the pump is the mechanical seal on the shaft between the motor and the pump. This seal keeps water out of the motor so the motor will stay dry. More expensive pumps have a spring-loaded seal of ceramic and carbon. This type of seal can be replaced if necessary.

The most important thing to remember about installing the water pump is that it should be placed in a cool, clean, and dry location. Make sure it is protected from leaves or other debris that could clog the cooling or ventilation slots in the motor. Also keep the pump away from a laundry room vent that emits lint from a clothes dryer.

The best pump location is in a waterproof enclosure with louvers for cross-ventilation. This type of installation may be required to comply with the manufacturer's warranty.

Filters, Purifiers, and Skimmers

The filter and skimmer make up the filtration system that keeps the spa water clean. The skimmer removes large floating objects, such as leaves, from the surface before allowing the water to enter the filter for cleaning. The filter removes most, but not all, unwanted substances that are suspended in the water. In order to operate efficiently, the filter must be matched to the water pump and spa size. If the water pump is too powerful, it will push the water through the filter too fast. As a result, the filter will not work effectively and may even sustain damage.

The warm water of a spa is a natural breeding ground for bacteria, algae, and other contaminants. The people using the spa introduce bacteria, dirt, skin particles, and body oils to the spa water. These pollutants reduce the clarity of the water and change its color and odor. Because of these conditions the spa water must be correctly sanitized at all times.

The biggest enemies of the filter are body oil, suntan oil, lotions, and creams. These materials will form a film over the filtering material and cause premature filter clogging. You can reduce this problem by showering before entering the water. Sun protection products should be nonoily.

Filter Types

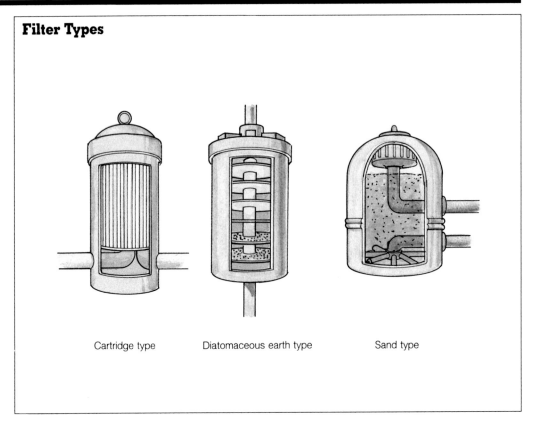

Cartridge type   Diatomaceous earth type   Sand type

Cartridge Filter

The cartridge filter is used with most home spas. Public spas or very large home spas usually use diatomaceous earth (DE) or sand filters because they can handle a greater volume of water and a heavier dirt load.

The cartridge filter is made of treated fiber, either Dacron or a nonwoven polyester, and is accordion-pleated and capped at each end, like some automotive air and oil filters. This pleating creates a large surface area within a small cylinder. The larger surface area allows a greater volume of water to flow through the filter.

The filter traps dirt before the water enters the pump and heater, keeping both units clean. This type of filter has to be removed routinely and cleaned, by using a garden hose and plenty of water, to flush out the dirt buildup. Be sure to rinse out any embedded dirt in the creases. If these areas are overlooked, the filter will become clogged sooner and may be damaged. If the filter has been neglected or is severely clogged, soak it in a special cleaning fluid recommended by the filter manufacturer, then rinse it thoroughly.

The more often the spa is used, and the more people who use the spa, the more often the filter will have to be cleaned. The timing for filter service is something you will learn after

prolonged use of the spa. A high-quality cartridge filter usually will last one to two years if it is properly maintained by routine thorough cleaning.

The material used in cartridge filters cleans the water sufficiently for home use. Although it is not as effective as a DE filter or a sand filter, the cartridge filter is much easier to maintain.

Diatomaceous Earth Filter

The diatomaceous earth (DE) filter is used primarily in public and residential swimming pools, as well as in very large spas or swim spas. Diatomaceous earth is an excellent filtering agent and is best suited for a large volume of water with a heavy dirt load.

The diatomaceous earth used in the filters comes from a soft rock, found mainly in the western states, which consists of the fossilized remains of sea organisms (diatoms). These rocks are pulverized into a very fine, chalky powder, which is then applied to pads within the DE filter grid.

DE filters are cleaned by back-flushing the filter with the spa water. The amount of water necessary to properly back-flush a DE filter may be the total amount of water contained in the spa.

This wastewater then must be discharged and the spa refilled with fresh water. After the DE filter is back-flushed, it must be recoated with new diatomaceous earth.

Sand Filter

The sand filter contains a large volume of sand in the base of the filter housing. The dirty water enters the filter at the top. The water percolates through the sand, depositing the dirt and debris in the sand, where it is trapped. The water then leaves through the bottom of the filter housing cleaned.

When the sand eventually becomes dirty, the water flow is restricted. The filter must then be cleaned by back-flushing the filter with the spa water. As with the DE filter, the amount of water necessary to back-flush a sand filter properly may be the total

amount of water in the spa. After back-flushing, the wastewater must be discharged and the spa refilled with fresh water.

Each filter manufacturer recommends a specific type and size of sand to be used in the particular filter. The wrong type or size of sand will greatly reduce filter effectiveness.

Ultraviolet Water Sterilizer

Ultraviolet light has long been used to sterilize medical equipment, and it is sometimes used to sterilize spa water. An ultraviolet bulb is encased in a waterproof container and placed in the water-flow system. As the water flows past the unit, the ultraviolet rays change the oxygen particles in the water into ozone, killing unwanted organisms.

Ultraviolet sterilization eliminates the need for chlorine- or bromine-based compounds and creates no chemical odor. In some cases a hydrogen peroxide–based solution is added to the water as a sanitizer. This solution should be matched to the manufacturer's sterilizer unit so everything is compatible.

An ultraviolet sterilizer usually can sanitize the spa water by operating for only a couple of hours a day at about the cost of running a medium-sized light bulb.

The water is sterilized only when it passes the ultraviolet bulb unit in the circulation equipment. The ultraviolet system works well, but it is not as effective as a chlorine or bromine solution, which kills off microorganisms as soon as they enter the spa water.

Ionizer

The water ionization system was used to purify water as early as the 1930s and was then refined and updated by NASA in the early 1960s to purify and recycle water for the astronauts in the Apollo spacecraft. An ionizer unit kills bacteria and algae by introducing an electric current between two metal electrodes, one of copper and the other of silver or stainless steel, located in the water-pipe system.

As the water passes between these two charged electrodes, the copper electrode kills algae and the silver or stainless-steel electrode kills bacteria. The bacteria and algae are then removed by the filter. Both of these sanitizing actions can also be accomplished with the use of chlorine.

The ionizer works harder when more electric current is applied to the electrodes. If the ionizer works too hard, the spa surface may be stained. However, the units available today are fully automatic and adjust to the correct level of current to purify a given amount of spa water.

The ionizer is an expensive piece of equipment, but it does eliminate 90 percent of the

need for chemicals normally required to treat spa water. Since the need to purchase chemicals is drastically reduced, the ionizer will pay for itself in about two years.

If the ionizer is equipped with copper and silver electrodes, the unit can be placed on either side of the filter, but to keep the unit cleaner, place it downstream from the filter. If the ionizer is equipped with copper and stainless-steel electrodes, it should be placed upstream from the filter. In this way, the minerals plated onto the electrodes will be trapped in the filter and not discharged into the spa. The ionizer must be wired into the power panel of the spa and should be incorporated into its filtration cycles.

Even with the use of the ionizer, some chemicals should still be used in the system. The pH factor and alkalinity level must still be maintained to keep the spa water healthful and balanced, since the ionizer does not maintain these parts of the water chemistry. Ask the ionizer manufacturer to recommend the correct amount of chemicals for your spa.

The size of the ionizer must be matched to the volume of water in your spa in order to perform at its best. The electrodes of the ionizer eventually wear out with use and must be replaced.

Ozone Generator

The ozone generator converts oxygen in the air to ozone and introduces it into the spa water. This method of swimming pool sanitation has been used in Europe for years and is one of the strongest oxidizing systems commercially available. It makes the water crystal clear, with very little chemical odor.

The ozone generator is an expensive piece of equipment, but it will reduce the time and money spent on adding chemicals normally required to treat the water. Depending on the size of the spa, the ozone generator will pay for itself in about two years.

As with ionizers, the pH factor and alkalinity must still be maintained by using chemicals.

The size of the ozone generator must be matched to the volume of water in the spa in order to reach its maximum level of efficiency.

Skimmer

The skimmer removes floating debris from spa water to prevent clogging of the drains, filter, and plumbing. The skimmer is built into the side of the spa at the waterline and is usually made of a noncorrosive plastic. As water and debris pass through the skimmer weir, particles are filtered into a plastic mesh basket. The basket is then removed from the skimmer and emptied.

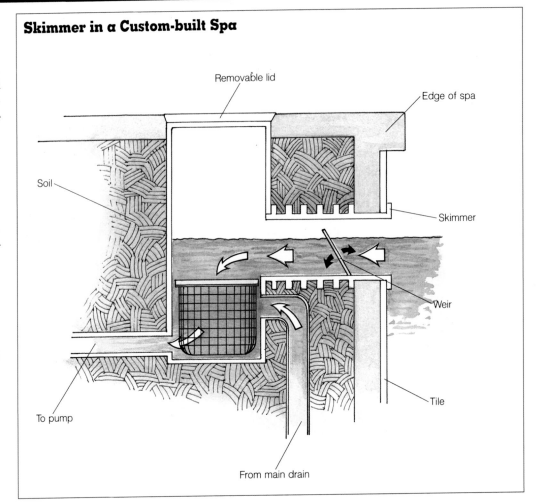

Skimmer in a Custom-built Spa

Removable lid

Edge of spa

Soil

Skimmer

Weir

Tile

To pump

From main drain

The skimmer basket should be emptied daily, or more often if there are a lot of leaves falling in the spa area. If the skimmer basket becomes clogged, it will restrict water outflow which could lead to water-pump damage.

The weir flap on the front of the skimmer is a critical part of the unit and must operate properly. The weir floats on the water surface, allowing only water and surface debris into the skimmer. The weir must pivot freely to work correctly; never let it become jammed with debris.

Water Heater

The water heater is one of the most important parts of the support equipment. Aside from the basic ergonomics of the spa, water temperature is what makes the spa comfortable. When considering the size of the heater, always choose a heater with a slightly higher BTU rating than necessary. It is better to have a heater that is a little larger than is required than to be stuck with a small one that never heats the water to the preferred temperature quickly. To keep the water at the desired temperature, a small heater will have to run longer and will waste more energy than a larger one that doesn't have to operate as long. On the other hand, it is a waste of money to buy a heater that is too large.

Spa heaters are usually of the rapid recovery type, in which water is recirculated and reheated continuously.

The equipment for this built-in spa is securely housed in a permanent enclosure, which blends in with the surrounding deck.

BTU Rating and Heater Size

Choosing the correct size heater with the right BTU rating is a must when you choose your support equipment. The heat produced by the heater is measured in British thermal units, or BTUs, generated in one hour. One BTU is the energy required to raise 1 pound of water 1° Fahrenheit. All heaters are rated in BTUs and have a rating tag attached to them with all of the necessary data listed on it.

The size of the heater you choose depends on how fast you want to heat your spa. Most spa owners want to be able to use their spa within one hour.

The salesperson can tell you how long it will take to heat the spa water to the desired temperature with the standard-BTU-rated water heater. If you feel the warm-up time is not satisfactory, consider purchasing the optional higher-BTU-rated heater.

If you plan to buy the optional higher-output water heater, do so at the very beginning. It is less expensive to include the higher-BTU-rated water heater at the start than to add it later. If an optional heater is added later, the electrical system may have to be enlarged because of the higher amperage requirements, or a natural gas line may have to be added.

Are you going to heat the spa in cold weather? An indoor spa can be used the year around with a minimal change

in the fuel bill, but if you are going to use an outdoor spa during cold weather, be sure to have a heater large enough to manage the temperature change—and be prepared for an increase in fuel consumption. An outdoor spa can be used during cold weather as long as the spa and water pipes are well insulated and an equally well-insulated cover is placed over the spa when it is not in use.

A word of caution: If the spa is not drained for the winter, do not use the heater to try to prevent the spa water from freezing; if a heater is used for a long period of time to maintain the water temperature at 70° F or less, the heater will

sustain damage. Spa winterizing is covered in the fifth chapter (page 108).

Calculating the Correct Heater Size

A reputable spa dealer can recommend the correct size heater for your spa. Most portable spas are equipped with an electric heater matched to that specific spa, but you can choose a higher BTU rating. Heaters for built-in spas should be individually matched to the spa.

Refer to the manufacturer's literature for BTU ratings and specifications. There should be a chart indicating how long it will take to raise the spa water temperature 10° F. The chart will list the water capacity for each size spa.

Types of Heaters

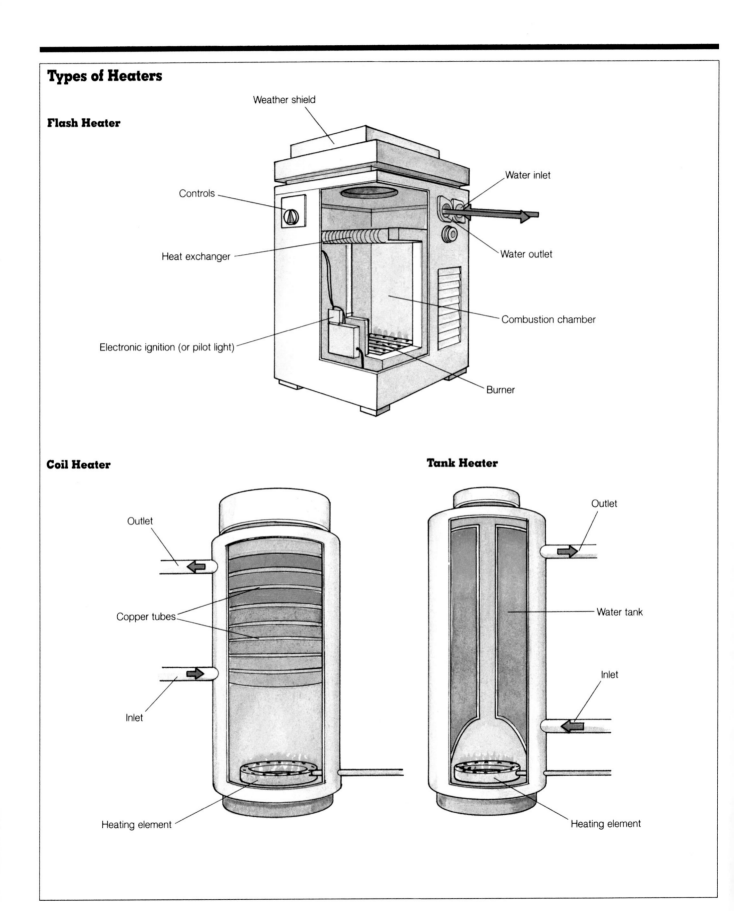

Flash Heater

Weather shield

Controls

Heat exchanger

Electronic ignition (or pilot light)

Water inlet

Water outlet

Combustion chamber

Burner

Coil Heater

Outlet

Copper tubes

Inlet

Heating element

Tank Heater

Outlet

Water tank

Inlet

Heating element

With a fossil-fuel heater rated at 5,000 BTUs, it will take 33 minutes for a 10° F increase, so it will take 1 hour and 39 minutes for a temperature increase of 30° F. It would take an 11.5-kilowatt electric heater to increase the water temperature in the same amount of time.

Types of Heaters

For larger spas and swim spas, a fossil-fuel heater is usually less expensive to operate than an electric heater. Smaller portable spas are ordinarily equipped with an electric heater, mainly because a smaller volume of water is being heated.

Fossil-Fuel Heater

A fossil-fuel heater can run on natural gas, propane, or fuel oil. The choice of fuel depends on what is available in your area and which is the least expensive to use. Some heaters can be adapted to run on any of the three types, while other heaters are designed for one specific fuel.

The best and most common type of fossil-fuel heater is the flash heater. This type uses a large burner to warm the heat exchanger unit. The heat exchanger unit has copper pipes running back and forth within it that carry the water. The copper pipes are equipped with fins that pick up the heat quickly and transfer it to the water running through them. The flow rate of the water depends on the diameter of the copper pipes and the capacity of the water pump.

Many of the newer spa heaters are equipped with an electronic ignition system, which eliminates the need for an energy-consuming pilot light. Some even include a remote control that allows you to turn on an outdoor-spa heater from inside the house.

Flash heaters are very efficient and are best suited for spas; they have been used to heat swimming pools for many years. The heater can be installed outdoors, or indoors if building codes allow it.

Avoid the tank type of heater, which is similar in construction to a household water heater. This type of heater is not suited for spa use because it does not heat water on demand and does not maintain the water temperature efficiently.

The most important aspect of a fossil-fuel heater is that it has been manufactured to the specifications of and is certified by the American Gas Association (AGA).

Electric Heater

An electric heater is usually smaller than a fossil-fuel heater and is used primarily in small and portable spas. The electric heater is not as energy efficient and usually takes longer than a fossil-fuel heater to bring the water to the desired temperature.

If an electric heater is used, you should leave it on to maintain the water at the ideal temperature. If the heater is turned off, the reheating time is quite lengthy, considerably longer than with a fossil-fuel heater.

The initial cost of an electric heater is usually less than that of a fossil-fuel heater. Electric heaters are available for both 110-volt and 220-volt hookups.

The construction of the electric heater is very important. The electric heater should have corrosion-resistant metals in both the heating element and the housing. The insulation should be of a nonasbestos material similar to the calcium silicate that is commonly used to insulate steam pipes.

Electric heaters have a loop or coil heating element, or both types, within the heater housing. The water flows through this chamber, passes by the heated element, and is heated. The flow rate of the water depends on the diameter of the inlet and outlet pipes and the capacity of the water pump.

The most important point to look for in an electric heater is that it has been manufactured to the specifications of and is certified by the Underwriters' Laboratory (UL) Standard 1261 for indoor/outdoor electric heaters.

Solar Heater

Solar heating is really not as suited to spas as it is to swimming pools. Heating a pool that uses lower temperature water by tapping the power of the sun has become quite cost-effective in many areas. Many states offer a tax break for those

who use solar heating, helping to offset the cost of a solar heating system.

The desired water temperature for a spa is about 20° F higher than that of a swimming pool. This warmer temperature is difficult to obtain with solar heating unless you live in a very sunny climate. If you do choose to install solar panels for heating the spa, you should also have a backup system—usually an electric heater—for cloudy days and for times when solar heating does not bring the water up to the desired temperature.

Two basic types of solar collector panels are available. The less expensive type consists of unglazed plastic panels. These panels contain black plastic, rubber, or composition rubber tubing or channels. This kind of construction is called unglazed because the panels are not covered with glass or clear plastic. Rolls of black tubing are also used. Because the panels do not greatly increase the water temperature, plastic PVC (polyvinyl chloride) pipe can be used to connect the solar panels to the support equipment. This type of system usually will not provide the same increase in water temperature as glazed (glass-covered) panels do, and it also requires a larger panel area.

Single-glazed or double-glazed collector panels are more efficient but are also more expensive. This type of solar

Solar Heating System

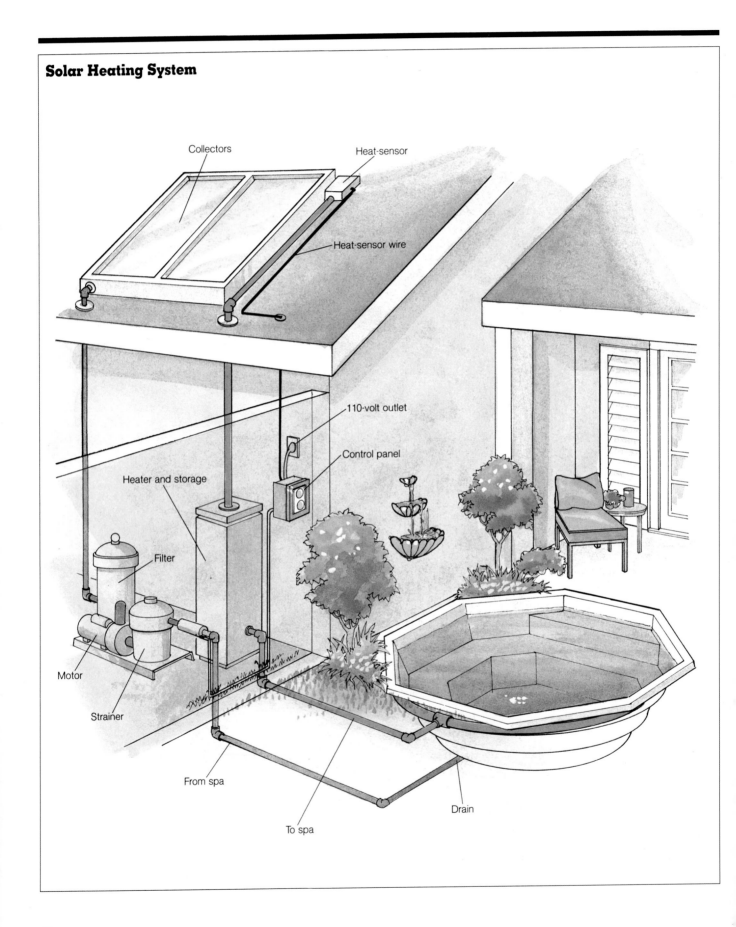

Collectors

Heat-sensor

Heat-sensor wire

110-volt outlet

Control panel

Heater and storage

Filter

Motor

Strainer

From spa

To spa

Drain

heating system is now used primarily for home water-heating systems or for swimming pools. Because it produces the highest water temperature increase, it is better suited than an unglazed system for the spa. Because of the higher temperature generated by the glazed panels, copper plumbing is usually required to connect the solar panels to the rest of the support equipment.

If you already have a solar heating system for home water use or for an existing swimming pool, you may be able to integrate the existing system with the spa or modify it to handle the additional load.

If you are thinking about using solar heating, consult with a solar-energy professional; the technology is changing rapidly. Talk with dealers who carry both the unglazed and glazed systems and have them explain which system is best suited to your needs.

Cost of Running a Heater

The cost of running a spa heater depends on your climate, the relative cost of different energy sources, how often the spa is used, and whether the water will be heated constantly or reheated each time the spa is used.

Most spa or spa heater manufacturers will include in their sales and technical literature the cost of running the heater for each specific spa.

Frequency of spa use will greatly affect your fuel bill. If the spa will be used every day and is heated electrically, it is best to maintain the spa temperature because the electric heater takes a relatively long time to bring the water temperature up. If a fossil-fuel heater is used, it can be turned off between soaks because it can heat the spa water on demand more quickly.

Air Blowers

Air blowers are used to agitate the spa water gently with clouds of tingling bubbles. Air channels are attached to the outer surface of the spa shell, and small holes are drilled through the spa floor into these channels. An electric blower directs air through the air channels and out through the holes. This system is quite simple and is usually trouble free.

The one disadvantage is heat loss from the bubble action. Each bubble that travels through the warm water and then breaks at the surface expels a small amount of heat along with the air. If the ambient air temperature is on the cool side, the water temperature can drop quickly.

The best type of air-blower motor is the bypass type, which has its own cooling fan. The motor must be kept cool, especially if it is located under the skirt of a portable spa.

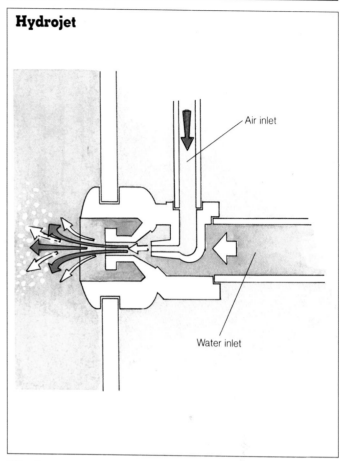

Hydrojet

Air inlet

Water inlet

Hydrojets

Hydrojets are used to agitate the water and provide a relaxing massage action by pushing and swirling a mixture of water and air. The hydrojet pumps water from a large-diameter pipe through a smaller-diameter pipe, causing a venturi action. This venturi action increases the water pressure and also creates a vacuum in which air is sucked into the water stream, creating an air-and-water mixture.

The number and placement of the hydrojets is usually determined by spa manufacturers. Over the years they have

found the most logical and beneficial locations for the hydrojets. Some spa manufacturers will allow you to add, remove, or relocate the hydrojets. The only way to know if you like the placement of the hydrojets is to take a "wet test" at the dealer in the exact model of spa that you plan to purchase. Only by actually feeling the hydrojets against your body will you know if you like the locations.

Some spa manufacturers offer hydrojets that can be adjusted to change the exit angle of the water and the proportions of water and air that come through the jets. In some spas, a valve can direct all of the hydrojet action to a single large jet at one end. This creates a swirling action that can be directed toward any part of your body. This single outlet of high-pressure water has a great therapeutic value.

One major spa manufacturer has a hydrojet that moves vertically. With this system, known as a perpetually reciprocating jet, you can get your back massaged without moving in the spa. The jet-flow rate is also adjustable.

Plumbing and Fittings

Unless otherwise specified by local building and plumbing codes, all hot and cold water lines, drain lines, and air lines can be plumbed with rigid or flexible polyvinyl chloride (PVC) pipe and fittings. This type of pipe is very easy to work with, and if the joints are properly connected with the appropriate primer and glue, it will provide a firm watertight seal. The pipe and all types of fittings are available at most hardware stores or plumbing-supply houses. Very little skill is required to work with PVC pipe and its related fittings. These techniques are covered in the fourth chapter (pages 84 to 86).

The standards for PVC pipe type, size, and wall thickness are determined by your local building code. Check the code before purchasing any of these plumbing components. Some building departments will allow the use of special PVC

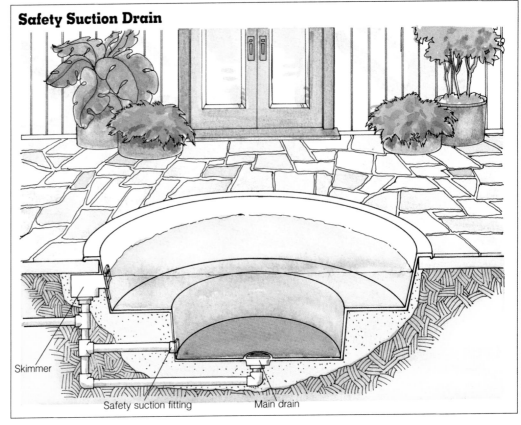

Safety Suction Drain

Skimmer

Safety suction fitting

Main drain

pipes and fittings for natural gas lines. In some areas, the natural gas lines must have special protective wrapping because of soil conditions.

Due to the heat generated by a spa heater, most manufacturers of fossil-fuel heaters require that copper pipe be used on both the inlet and outlet sides of the heater for a specified distance. This is necessary to dissipate the heat generated by the heater. There are plumbing fittings that allow copper pipe to be joined to PVC pipe.

Make sure plastic plumbing fittings have plumbing code approval, such as an IAPMO seal on them. This will ensure that the parts have been manufactured in accordance with strict specifications.

Drains and Suction Fittings

Because the spa water is recirculated, there must be one or more drains and suction fittings to evacuate the water from the spa and return it to the filter and heater.

Usually there is one main drain in the spa located at the lowest point. This is desirable so when the spa is drained for cleaning, all of the water can be expelled before adding new water. The drain must be covered with a protective anti-vortex cover. This cover prevents whirlpool action as the water drains and helps to avoid hair entanglement. Some building codes require the spa to have a secondary drain mounted on the side away from the main drain in the

floor. With two drains, there is less suction at each one, thereby reducing the possibility of hair entanglement.

Controls

All portable spas, and some smaller built-in spas, have a control panel that is integrated into the spa. In most cases the supplied control panel is the only one available with that particular spa.

If you have a choice, opt for simple mechanical controls. These have been proven reliable over the years, are durable, and are easy to service when necessary. Stay away from push-button controls and digital readouts, if possible, as they are

Antivortex Drain

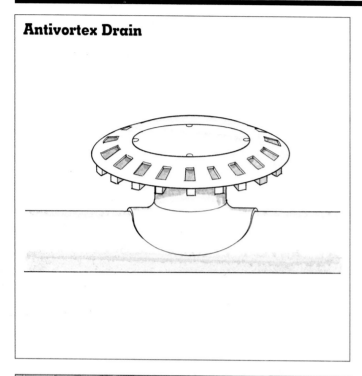

This portable spa, located in a newly built basement room, includes a built-in equipment enclosure. The spa cover reduces heat loss and evaporation into the room.

more prone to problems and are more expensive to service.

Some spa manufacturers offer controls that are operated by cables or air pressure so there is no voltage at the control unit. This eliminates any possibility of electric shock. The control panel should have a lockable cover. If the cover is secured, no one can change the controls without the person in charge of the spa knowing about it. This feature also makes the controls childproof.

A timer that will turn the pump and heater on at a predetermined time is a handy feature. This way you can come home and get right into the preheated water for a relaxing hot soak.

Automatic controls can also be installed to turn on various parts of the spa support equipment at predetermined times. These controls can regulate the heater or turn on the water pump to circulate the water. Some automatic controls have a remote feature that allows you to control the equipment of an outdoor spa from inside the house.

When choosing controls, make sure that they are designed specifically for swimming pools or spas and that they have the UL seal of approval.

Covers

The spa cover is the most important item for energy conservation. With the cover in place, heat loss will be kept to a minimum as will water and chemical evaporation. Some states will even give a tax credit on the purchase price of the spa cover. A well-insulated

cover reduces the heating time and may even pay for itself within one year, due to smaller energy bills.

The cover also prevents dirt and debris from falling into an outdoor spa. For an indoor spa, the cover is used primarily to reduce heat loss and water evaporation as well as to keep the humidity level in the room to a minimum.

There are two basic types of spa covers: rigid and flexible. If child protection is a priority, the rigid cover is the type to purchase. Flexible covers perform well in keeping out dirt and preventing evaporation and heat loss, but most will not prevent the accidental entry of a small child or animal.

Rigid Cover

A rigid cover is usually more expensive than a flexible cover, but it has many advantages. It provides insulation, prevents water and chemical evaporation, keeps small children and pets from falling in, and keeps dirt and debris out of outdoor spas. Some of the better rigid covers can be locked in place, which provides peace of mind since the spa is child-proof when the cover is installed.

A rigid cover, if well maintained, will last a long time. It must be cleaned inside and out, and if it is made of a hard surface like Rovel® thermoplastic, it must be waxed periodically. If you have just added chemicals to the spa, wait about 30 minutes to an hour before installing the cover to allow some of the fumes to dissipate. If the cover is installed too soon, the inner surface may start to deteriorate.

Flexible Cover

A flexible cover is the least expensive kind of covering and prevents dirt, leaves, and debris from getting into the spa water. Some covers are made of polyethylene sheets with built-in air cells, similar to bubble-type packing material. The air cells allow the cover to float. If the spa is in a sunny location, a transparent cover can be used as a solar collector and can actually heat the water during sunlight hours. These covers do not perform as well if the spa is located in a shady place.

There is also a flexible closed-cell foam insulating cover that can be used either by itself or in conjunction with a rigid cover to reduce heat loss.

Another type of flexible cover is polypropylene mesh, which is similar to the shade cloth used in patio coverings but much stronger. This type of cover is secured to the sides of the spa to hold it in place. Some mesh covers, if secured properly, meet the Emergency Standard Safety Performance Specifications to provide a protective barrier over any in-ground pool or spa.

Lighting

Lighting in and around the spa will set the mood for after-dark relaxation. Many spas come with built-in low-voltage lighting that can change the color of the water to set different moods, from a cool blue or

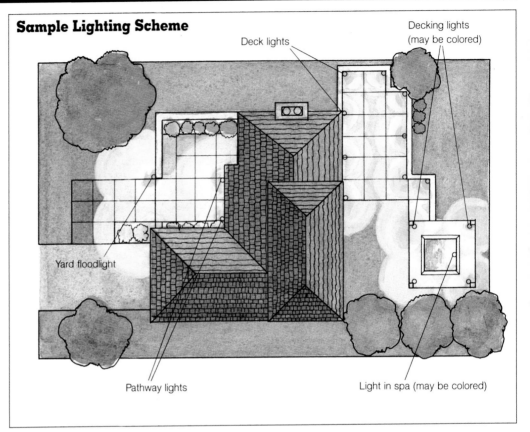

Sample Lighting Scheme

Deck lights

Decking lights (may be colored)

Yard floodlight

Pathway lights

Light in spa (may be colored)

green for relaxing, to a warm red or violet for fun and talking with friends.

The area around an outdoor spa should also be well lighted. Illuminate the pathway leading to the spa so it is safe at night for walking back and forth from the spa to the house. Be sure to light any hazardous areas, such as steps or deck edges. The lighting in the area immediately surrounding the spa should be controlled by a dimmer switch. This will allow you to switch from bright lighting for safety to low lighting for relaxation.

Energy-saving low-voltage lighting sets are available from most hardware stores and can be used for mood lighting in the area surrounding the spa. Keep this type of lighting low to the ground so it will be diffused and subtle. Some of

the lights can be placed in or next to plants or trees in the landscaping.

All of the lighting equipment must be UL approved and the lighting circuit must be protected by a GFCI circuit breaker.

Accessories

Even though the spa is not as large as a swimming pool, there are some scaled-down swimming pool items that can be used in a spa. Anything from floating vinyl pillows and inflatable creatures for the kids to floating food trays and thermometers can add entertainment and practical value to the spa. These items are available at pool and spa-supply stores as well as many sporting goods outlets and toy stores.

Covered headrests are also available in materials that will not be damaged by the spa water. These add greatly to the comfort of the spa while lounging.

There are even fragrances that can be added to the water to give it a pleasing scent, such as honeysuckle or forest pine. These fragrances are sold in liquid or crystal form and are formulated specifically for safe use in a spa. There is also an additive that can turn your spa into a natural mineral bath. These products are designed so they will not affect the pH balance of the water, clog the filter, or stain or discolor spa finishes. When purchasing one of these items, make sure it is safe for spa use. Don't add any other type of product because it may damage the support equipment.

COST CONSIDERATIONS

Spa selection offers a wide range of options, and every choice has its costs. This is an area in which research rewards the careful. Well-considered questions, and time spent with a pencil, paper, and calculator, can prevent surprises and bring benefits for years to come.

Built-In or Portable

Comparing the prices of built-in and portable spas brings up a lot of variables besides the initial price of the spa. Actual dollar amounts for the different components and services are not given here because the price of the spa, delivery and labor charges, landscaping, and interior decorating costs vary so much from region to region.

A built-in spa will usually cost more than a portable unit because of the amount of work involved in preparing the area for the spa shell. In most cases, a portable spa is the least expensive to purchase and install. If you want to enjoy hot soaking with a minimum outlay of money, the portable spa is ideal. For an exterior installation, the portable spa can be purchased, delivered, and placed on an existing strong deck or patio slab. If the portable spa is to be installed inside a home, some modifications to the room will be necessary. The portable spa is heavy after being filled with water, and the floor must be reinforced to accommodate this added weight. The room also must have water spillover protection and adequate ventilation to evacuate moisture and residual chemical odors.

In order for the spa to look as if it fits into its surroundings, the yard should be landscaped, with the possible addition of a deck, or the indoor room may have to be modified to integrate the spa into the decor. The price for these modifications is about the same for built-in or portable spas.

Suggestions for integrating either a built-in or portable spa into its surroundings are presented in detail in the first and second chapters.

If you are qualified, you can save a lot of money by installing the spa yourself. This may make it possible to purchase a more expensive spa and have more elaborate surroundings for the same price as a cheaper spa installed by professionals. Do-it-yourself installation is covered in the fourth chapter (page 94).

Heating Costs

The cost of running a spa averages about a dollar a day in most locations. However, the cost depends greatly on the size of the spa and how well it is insulated. Cost is also affected by climate, the distance of the heater from the spa, and use of an insulated cover. Your preferred water temperature will also affect the daily cost.

If the spa is located outdoors, in cold weather it will cost more to heat. Maximum recommended water temperature is 104° F (40° C) for adults, lower for children; most people will settle for a slightly lower, more comfortable water temperature. A lower water temperature allows you to stay in the spa and soak longer. Refer to the fifth chapter (page 105) for recommended water temperatures, soaking time, and safety tips.

An insulated cover will maintain the water temperature between uses at a minimum cost.

Financing

A variety of lending institutions can help you finance your spa and its installation. Before applying for a loan, estimate the cost of the total installation. This includes the spa and support equipment as well as landscaping and decks for an outdoor spa or building modifications for an indoor spa. Don't cut yourself short by financing just the spa unit; you may not have sufficient funds to complete the job.

Loans for spas are usually the same as for swimming pools and most often fall into the home-improvement category. This type of loan is usually considered a personal loan, since there is really no collateral. The loan isn't secured by the spa itself but by your good credit standing. If you have taken out a prior loan with the lending institution and paid it back on time with no problems, it will probably be happy to work with you again.

Be sure to shop around for the loan. Don't settle for the first one you find. This is time well spent, as you may be making payments on the loan for five to seven years, or even longer for a large project.

These are some sources to investigate for financing a spa.
• Banks. First, inquire at your present bank. Many banks will offer slightly less expensive loans to their existing customers. They may even arrange to have the payments automatically deducted from your checking or savings account.
• Credit unions. If you or your spouse belong to a credit union, be sure to check there also. In many cases credit unions can beat the interest percentage offered by other lending institutions.
• Home equity loan. Equity in your home can be used to finance your spa. Different types of home equity loans have different interest rates and tax consequences; obtain professional advice before choosing. Also, bear in mind that your house—probably your most valuable possession—is the collateral for this type of loan.

Insurance Coverage

Before you install a spa, notify your homeowner's or renter's insurance carrier. In most cases, homeowners can be covered under their existing policy. If you rent, coverage for the spa may be included in your renter's policy. Consult your agent.

An insurance agent will want to know about all the safety features of the spa and its surroundings and may even have some safety requirements that are necessary in order to add the spa to your existing policy.

HOW TO JUDGE DEALERS AND PRODUCTS

By offering quality products and sound advice at key moments, a reliable dealer can make an enormous difference in how well your spa project turns out.

How to Choose a Reliable Dealer

A good dealer usually is a full-service dealer. This is someone who can sell you the spa and support equipment and also has the ability to secure the necessary permits, install the spa or subcontract the installation, and service the equipment after installation. The dealer may even offer a landscaping service or recommend a landscape architect. This type of dealer will usually provide you with a package of services that will make the entire project less frustrating and more enjoyable.

A dealer who specializes in spas is more likely to be knowledgeable about the latest spa technology. The dealer should know about recent developments and be able to provide state-of-the-art equipment. Some spa manufacturers also build swimming pools, and some dealers may represent both products. If you choose a dealer with a dual-product line, make sure the dealer fully understands spas and doesn't consider them just a sideline.

Check to see that the dealer sells name-brand spas, support equipment, and accessories, and make sure the support equipment is approved by the appropriate standards organizations, such as Underwriters' Laboratory.

When choosing a dealer, it helps to ask a lot of questions. Determine how long the dealer has been in business at the same location and under the same business name.

Ask the dealer for references from previous customers, then verify the references; if possible, look at their spas. Would you be satisfied with the work that was performed? Don't focus on the aesthetics of the installation, since personal tastes vary. Look at the care that has gone into the work and the details of the installation. Ask the owners how the spa has performed. If they had problems, find out how the dealer handled them.

Also ask them, "Would you work with this dealer again?"

Check with the local Better Business Bureau to see if there have been any complaints registered against the dealer. This is one of the best ways to judge a dealer's past performance.

Comparison Shopping

Don't jump into purchasing a spa from the first dealer you meet. This is just like buying an automobile from the first dealer you visit—without a test drive. This chapter gives you some idea of what to look for in a spa, but do shop around and become familiar with the products that are available. In order to save time, find a spa dealer who has a good selection and represents spas and support equipment made by different manufacturers. This will allow you to compare the same features on several different spas at one location.

Look at and try out as many spas as possible. A good dealership will offer you a "wet test" on an appointment basis, and some even have private areas where their spas are filled with hot water for testing. Sitting in an empty spa is completely different than sitting in one filled with hot water.

As mentioned earlier, home remodeling shows are an excellent source of information. You can also check the yellow pages for spa dealers in your area.

If you are not in a real hurry, go to the library and peruse the home-improvement magazines for spa manufacturers who offer brochures. Most of the literature is free, so send for it and see what types of spas are offered.

How to Judge the Finished Product

The only way to judge the quality of a spa and its support equipment is to carefully look over the finished product. Do a very thorough inspection because you are making a major investment. Check the interior area where you sit for fit and finish; then inspect the exterior, where all of the mechanical, electrical, and plumbing fixtures are located. On portable spas, it is difficult to examine the exterior components because polyurethane foam insulation usually covers most or all of them.

If the spa is portable, ask how thick the wood skirting is. The wood thickness can vary from ⅜ inch to ¾ inch. Make sure all doors are hung straight and are supported by strong hinges, and see that all controls are easily accessible and are covered with a lockable door.

After carefully inspecting the interior and exterior, ask questions about the spa and related components. Inquire about the R-rating of the insulation. Does the entire unit carry the IAPMO seal of approval? Are all of the electrical components UL approved? If a gas heater is used, is it AGA approved? Ask how many years the manufacturer has been in business and if it has manufactured spas all of that time. Many spa manufacturers were in the swimming pool business before making spas, and some still are. They may have been in business for 20 years but have been making spas for only the last two or three. Ask specific questions and get specific answers. Don't accept responses that are questionable or vague.

Talk with a few spa or swimming pool service companies in your area and inquire whether they have had any problems with the specific spa and support equipment that you are thinking of purchasing. If they have had complaints, try to discover what the problems are. After finding out,

What a Contract Should Include

Rule Number 1 in any type of contract is: "If it's not written in the contract, the dealer is not obligated to deliver it." Keep this important point in mind, not only in the purchase contract for the spa and the support equipment, but also for the spa installation if it is to be done by a contractor. Installation contracts are covered in the fourth chapter (pages 76 to 78).

Everything that the dealer has promised you during the sales presentation must be in writing. Never rely on some-one's word that he or she will provide you with something—make sure it is written down. Make sure all components that you buy are listed in the contract by manufacturer name, exact model number, capacity or rating, and any other important descriptions. Many kinds of equipment are available in today's spa market, and they differ in quality and price.

Make sure that you receive a copy of the warranty for each piece of equipment and that it specifies the exact model number, manufacturer, and so on.

Know the length of time for which each item is guaran-teed—never assume anything.

If you are purchasing the spa and support equipment di-rectly from a dealer on an in-stallment plan, make sure the schedule of payments is in-cluded. This should list the ex-act amount of each payment, the number of payments, and the total cost of the completed transaction including princi-pal, interest, and any loan fees.

The contract should also in-clude the exact date on which the spa and support equipment will be delivered, as well as the address to which it will be delivered.

Some dealers offer an "af-ter-installation" checkup to make sure that everything is operating correctly and that you are happy with the com-plete package. Take advantage of this offer if it is available.

Read and reread the con-tract. If possible, have someone else read it to ensure all the "legalese" means exactly what you agreed to verbally with the salesperson. Remember, have everything written down.

---

ask the service company or spa dealer if these problems have been corrected and, if so, ask for proof.

After you have gone through all of these tests and questions with one dealership and the spas it represents, re-peat the process with other dealers. This is a long but worthwhile process.

Warranty Protection

The warranties for the spa and equipment are very important.

Ask to see the written war-ranties that come with each piece of equipment and thor-oughly read each one. If you have any questions, be sure to ask the dealer and have all of the details explained. Also ask what responsibilities the owner has in order to keep the war-ranties in effect. If the spa is not maintained properly or is abused in any way, the warran-ties may be void.

The various materials used in spa-shell construction are warranted for different periods of time. The length of time generally depends on how long these materials have held up against deterioration.

Find out how any surface imperfections will be corrected. Will they be repaired by the dealer's service department or by a factory representative? What is the usual turnaround time on a warranty-related ser-vice complaint? Ask if the man-ufacturer will repair a major flaw in the shell surface or re-place the entire shell. This is important because a large blis-ter or crack may cause a leak.

The actual construction of the portable spa is usually war-ranted for about five years. Again, this depends on the manufacturer and the quality of the spa. A permanently in-stalled spa may not be covered in this manner because the spa will settle after installation and use. Sometimes the spa manu-facturer will warrant the struc-ture only if the manufacturer was responsible for the spa in-stallation; if it was done by the owner or another installer, it may not be covered.

Support equipment warran-ties are usually provided by the equipment manufacturers, not the spa manufacturer. A good warranty should cover both parts and labor. Ask the dealer how long the manufacturer has been in business and how it will handle any problems. Do these manufacturers have a ser-vice division or does the owner have to remove the defective equipment and send it in for repair or replacement? If you are not a do-it-yourselfer, avoid purchasing equipment with a warranty that would require you to remove and replace a failed component.

Complaint Resolution

Thorough research and a well-written contract will provide the best protection against complaints.

However, if you have a problem with a spa dealer or contractor who is a member of the National Spa and Pool In-stitute, let the institute know about the problem. The NSPI attempts to regulate its mem-bers to uphold the industry standards, and it has a commit-tee to investigate complaints.

The Better Business Bureau (BBB) is also an agency de-signed to help protect the pub-lic from unfair business practices. Call the BBB in your area to find out how to present your complaint. Some larger of-fices have a telephone com-plaint line to offer guidance on specific problems; others will simply ask your name and ad-dress and send you the neces-sary forms.

INSTALLING THE SPA

Once you have chosen a spa and carefully selected its location, it's time to install it. This chapter, along with the manufacturer's instructions, will guide you through all the steps required to install a spa. The process of installation is similar whether the spa will be installed indoors or outdoors, except that an outdoor spa may require an excavation, whereas an indoor spa will require floor and foundation modifications. The information in this chapter pertains to both types of installation; where indoor and outdoor installation procedures vary, the differences are described. If you are handy with tools and have the tools required, have good basic home-maintenance ability and can handle basic plumbing, you should be able to install the spa by yourself. Of course, you will need the help of a few friends.

In the tradition of the old-fashioned barn raising, installing a spa can turn hard work into a social event.

INSTALLING THE SPA YOURSELF

This is a major project, but you may be able to do all or part of it yourself. If you read this section carefully and compare the requirements of the job with your abilities, you will be able to choose the right course of action.

What's Realistic?

This chapter deals with prefabricated spas that are delivered ready to be installed by the do-it-yourselfer. It does not cover the actual building of a shotcrete, gunite, or concrete-and-tile spa. Spas other than the prefabricated type are usually beyond the range of skills of the typical homeowner or do-it-yourselfer and are almost always contracted out and constructed by a spa or swimming pool builder.

Most spa manufacturers supply installation literature with diagrams and basic step-by-step instructions. However, each spa installation varies because of differences in spa design, equipment, code requirements, and site location.

The spa is bulky, awkward to handle, and expensive. Don't try to be a hero by installing it alone; you could damage all or part of the spa. In order to safely install the spa, you will need the help of some friends with strong backs. The size of the spa will determine how many assistants you will need. If the spa is to be installed partway or all the way in the ground, you will need assistance when it is time to place

it into the excavated area. Promise your assistants a spa-opening party when the job is done and the spa is full of hot, bubbling water.

Before you start installing the spa, read and reread this chapter as well as the manufacturer's installation instructions, and make sure you can manage the job yourself, with the assistance of your friends when needed. If you feel unsure about installing the spa yourself, consider having all or part of the job done by a contractor. It's better to call on a contractor in the beginning than to get halfway into the installation and decide the job is too big for you to complete. If the spa installation is partially completed, some contractors may not want to take on the job of finishing it.

If you are not sure of your skills but want to be part of the installation process, you may decide to split up the installation steps and have a contractor perform certain parts of the installation while you do the other parts. If you choose this type of arrangement, you can tell your friends that you installed the spa along with "a little help" from a contractor.

Don't be afraid to get the assistance of a professional. Although it may cost more, in

most cases it is money well spent. The one procedure that *must* be left to an expert is the electrical wiring and hookup. Do not try to do the electrical portion of the job by yourself; have it done by a licensed electrical contractor. Even most professional spa installers subcontract the electrical work because of the safety factor. If you install a PVC fitting that leaks water, it poses no hazard and can be fixed with no problem, but an electrical mistake can cause a deadly shock if something is wired wrong or if a wire is not correctly grounded. This chapter includes general information about spa electrical needs so you will know what is required.

Skills Needed for the Job

You can install a spa if you have the necessary tools and the ability to use them properly. If you have completed home-improvement projects in the past, have had no problems with them, and are happy with the end results, you will probably be able to install the spa yourself. The big question to ask yourself is, "Am I qualified to start—and finish—a spa installation job?" If you don't feel qualified in one area, such as plumbing, you can have this portion of the job done by a contractor. If you feel you are qualified, then use this book as a guide. Don't get in over your

head, though; if you get into a situation where you feel unsure, call for assistance either from the spa dealer or a qualified professional.

To be enjoyable, the spa must perform properly with no routine problems due to improper installation. If the installation doesn't go as you expected it to, you will always have the nagging feeling that you should have had it done by a professional.

If you are going to install the spa yourself, you should purchase the latest version of the book titled, "Uniform Swimming Pool, Spa and Hot Tub Code," published by the International Association of Plumbing and Mechanical Officials (IAPMO). This book contains the latest and most up-to-date code information relating to spa installation. The book is revised every year and contains the code definitions and material specifications for swimming pools, spas, and hot tubs. The building department nearest you will probably have a copy that you can look at and should be able to tell you where this book is available for purchase. You can also check a technical or building-industry bookstore.

Tools and Materials

A large number of typical home-improvement tools, as well as some special tools required for plumbing and concrete work, are required to install a spa.

The first step is excavation of the spa site. If the yard surface is fairly flat, leveling can be accomplished with hand shovels, some string and stakes, and a line level. In some cases a pick is handy if the soil is very hard or has a high clay content. If the excavation will be extensive, you should consider having it done by a contractor.

For foundation work you will need a wheelbarrow and a shovel or hoe to mix the concrete. If you don't have a wheelbarrow, you can use a heavy-gauge galvanized trash barrel for mixing concrete. Don't try this in a plastic trash can, even a heavy-duty one, as it will probably break and spill the concrete exactly where you don't want it. If there is much concrete work, consider renting an electric mixer from a tool rental outlet.

You will also need assorted sizes of lumber, nails, and a hammer or two to build any required forms. If a concrete pad is to be poured, you will need some tools designed specifically for cement work. These include wood floats in several sizes, an edging trowel, and a couple of sizes of steel finishing trowels.

For plumbing you will need tools designed for the type of plumbing materials you plan to use, either PVC or copper pipe. To work with rigid PVC pipe, you will need a PVC cutter tool or a fine-tooth backsaw or hacksaw with a minimum of 24 teeth per inch. A fine-tooth blade is necessary to achieve a clean cut on the pipe. You should also have a miter box to hold the pipe while you cut it

in order to get a square end. PVC pipe and fittings are connected using a solvent-type glue, so you will need PVC cleaner and primer, and PVC solvent cement. Some PVC fittings are threaded and require an application of silicone sealant to the threads to achieve a watertight joint. Some special plumbing fittings must be tightened by hand only, without the use of a wrench, and these fittings usually are shipped with instructions. Always read all the manufacturer's instructions carefully to avoid damage during installation.

Flexible PVC pipe requires a flexible PVC solvent cement specifically formulated for this type of pipe. Flexible PVC pipe should be cut with a very sharp knife; do not try to cut it with a backsaw or hacksaw as you will end up with a ragged cut, making it difficult to attach the pipe securely to its fittings.

Copper pipe can be cut with a tubing cutter or a fine-tooth hacksaw with a minimum of 24 teeth per inch. You will also need a small-diameter half-round fine-cut file or a reamer, sandpaper or steel wool, solder, noncorrosive solder flux, and a propane torch.

Other special tools may also be required. Ask the dealer if you will need specialized tools for any component or fitting on your spa. It may be possible to purchase the tools from the dealer. Some basic tools, such as a tape measure, a caulking gun for silicone seal, slip-joint pliers, and other ordinary home-improvement tools will also be handy.

Organization of the Job

Before starting, go over all aspects of the job. Make up a list of all the materials you will need and try to have them on hand. It's frustrating and a waste of time to stop and run to the spa dealer, lumberyard, or hardware store for some part that you forgot to purchase.

Have the job site organized from the very beginning; this will save a lot of time in the long run. Know exactly where everything is going to be installed; when materials are delivered, have them placed as close to their final location as possible. This is especially important for heavy items, such as lumber, cement, bricks, and landscaping rocks. However, don't place anything where it will interfere with installation.

When expensive parts are delivered, such as the spa and support equipment, carefully examine them to be sure they were not damaged during shipment. Also be sure that everything you sign for was shipped and nothing is missing. If there is visible damage, do not accept the merchandise, or have the delivery people note on the shipping bill that there was damage and have them describe it in detail. Once you sign the shipping bill acknowledging that you received the goods, the shipper is released from any responsibility. Any further damage will be assessed to you and not to the shipping company.

If possible, have finished-lumber deck material—or anything else that is sensitive to sunlight—placed in a shady area, or cover it. If you have room in the garage, store it inside, out of the elements. Direct sun may cause lumber to warp or buckle, which will make it difficult to work with during installation. Once the lumber is installed, the elements present no problem. Exposure is not as critical for construction-grade lumber, so it can be left exposed.

The interior of the spa is the finished surface that you will be sitting on, and it must be protected at all times. If the interior surface is not covered when the spa is shipped to you, cover it immediately. Use heavy plastic sheeting or cardboard, and secure it in place with duct tape. Do not apply the duct tape directly to the finished surface of the spa shell, as the tape will usually leave an adhesive residue when it is removed, especially if it has been exposed to direct sunlight. Attach the tape to the underside of the shell, if possible, and try to keep this covering in place until the spa is completely installed.

Whenever the spa is moved on the job site, be sure there are enough people to pick it up and move it carefully so it will not be damaged. Never drag the spa over the ground. Don't be tempted to carry the spa by the exposed plumbing pipes or fixtures. These pipes look like natural carrying handles, but the pipes or the spa shell may sustain damage if you use them for moving the spa.

HIRING A CONTRACTOR

You may decide that part of the job, or perhaps all of it, calls for professional help. Choosing the right contractor is vital; so is deciding which parts of the job to have done by a contractor. The following guidelines will help you make these decisions.

The Owner-Builder

There are two ways to hire professionals to install a spa: You can act as the contractor and hire subcontractors, such as an excavator, plumber, or electrician; or you can hire a contractor to organize and supervise all aspects of the spa installation.

If you decide to be the contractor, you are in essence the owner-builder, and you take on the responsibility of the entire job, from start to finish. By doing this, you can save the money that the general contractor usually makes on the job—but is it worth it in the long run? Your responsibilities may include such matters as taxes, workers' compensation, and other legal liabilities. You must also purchase all materials and schedule their arrival so the job continues smoothly. You will need to be at the job site most of the time to make sure everything is done correctly and to solve any problems that may arise. If you are unfamiliar with the construction industry and how it operates, it is better to have a contractor do the whole job.

How to Choose a Contractor

Most contractors are honest, hardworking, and financially responsible individuals, but, as in any type of business, there are those who bend the rules and try to take advantage of the public. Conduct the research for a contractor in much the same way you did for the spa and spa dealer; spend some time and do a thorough survey. The dealership from which you purchased your spa may have a regular contractor who installs its spas. Often, the dealer will have photographs representing typical spa installations by this contractor. Investigate this contractor first, since he or she was recommended.

Check with the Contractor's State Licensing Board to make sure the contractor is licensed and bonded. Also make sure the contractor carries workers' compensation insurance. You can also call the Better Business Bureau to look into the contractor's past performance.

Find out how long various contractors have been in business and how long they have been installing spas. A contractor may have been in business for 10 years but has been installing spas for just the last year and a half. Try to choose a contractor who has been installing spas for at least 5 to 10 years. The contractor should have appropriate credentials and a reputation not only for fast work but also for high-quality work. The contractor should use the most modern tools and techniques to do the job well and finish it on schedule.

Ask the contractor for references of completed spa installations, and get the names and telephone numbers of these customers. Contact them and ask if you can come over and look at their spa. If you are impressed with the installation, ask them if they would work with this contractor again.

How to Solicit and Judge Bids

Try to find a number of contractors you could work with and get a bid from each of them. You have the responsibility to furnish them with a detailed list of what you expect for your spa installation. Only by having this list will you be able to compare in detail the difference between the contractors' quoted prices.

Ask each contractor to submit a written bid detailing all materials and services that will be provided, and a cost breakdown for each step of the installation. After you receive the bids, check each one very carefully and make sure every item you requested is specified in detail on the bid. If something is not included, find out why it was deleted. Several missing or incorrect items on the contract may indicate that the contractor is disorganized. Scratch this person off of your list.

Ask each contractor how long the written bid will be honored. Since material and labor costs change frequently, the bid will be good for only a certain number of days or months. This is usually written on the bid, but if it is not, have the contractor put it in writing. You don't want to select a contractor and then find out that the bid is no longer valid.

In some cases the total dollar amount of the bids may vary drastically. If this happens, a good rule of thumb is to eliminate the high and low bidders and choose from the people in the middle. If all the contractors are from the same city or county, labor and material costs should be similar for all of them. The difference in the price quoted is then the contractor's overhead or profit margin. In some cases the price is negotiable, so if you are impressed with a particular contractor, ask if the job could be rebid at a lower price. You'll never know if you don't ask.

What an Agreement With a Contractor Should Contain

Everything that the contractor has included in the bid must be written into the contract. Never rely on someone's verbal promise to provide goods or services. If it is not written into a contract, you do not have any legal right to it.

Make sure the contract is written legally and that it complies with local laws. If possible, have a lawyer look it over to make sure all bases are covered and that the contract will stand up in court if any problems should arise.

This is a basic list of what should be in the contract.

• Exactly what will be performed, and by whom, should be clearly stated. If the contractor is going to use subcontractors for any part of the job, have the contractor list all of them by name and business address. Investigate all subcontractors just as you did the contractor.

• The language should specify the quality of the job. Don't settle for the usual contract jargon that the work is to be performed in "a workmanlike manner," which refers to the common trade practice of construction. You want a cut above this level of expertise, the level that is usually associated with a careful homeowner's standards.

• The approximate starting date should be specified.

• A completion date—with specific penalties if the project is not completed on time—should also be stated. In some contracts, the contractor must pay the owner a certain amount of money per day for each day past the completion date; in other cases, the owner may be obligated to pay the contractor the same dollar amount per day if the job is completed earlier than scheduled.

• A clause should state the dollar amount you must pay the contractor if you decide to cancel the project before it starts.

• Material specifications are to be given. These should include any applicable manufacturer's name, the exact model number, capacity or rating, etc. Specify everything, such as what type of wood or stone, or what concrete color, is to be used.

Careful planning will prevent surprises on installation day. This crane delivery, arranged in advance, makes light work of what would otherwise be a daunting task.

• Stipulations for any changes or additions should be included. Usually if the value of the change is above $100, it must be added to the contract in detail and initialed by both parties.

• A schedule of payments is necessary. Payments can be made when a specified percentage of the job is completed or at building code sign-off times. Always hold back the last payment until after the project is done and the building permit is signed off. If the job doesn't pass inspection and the contractor is paid in full, you have no leverage to get the contractor to correct the problem.

How to Work With a Contractor

For results, there must be co-operation between the owner and the contractor. Working on a large spa installation that may include decking and landscaping often involves making a lot of decisions along the way about things that may have been unforeseen. Once the project is started, the contractor may make suggestions to enhance the job or to save time or money. Be open to these ideas; they may benefit you in the long run. The contractor should also be flexible if you come up with suggestions for changes.

You should establish work hours and days for the contractor's crew. Check with your building department regarding

weekend work, as some communities regulate this. Establish how the workers will enter the yard or house, and decide if they are to have house refrigerator and bathroom privileges.

If you observe something that you don't like or feel is inappropriate, say so immediately. If you wait too long, it may be too late to change it. If you see one of the workers doing something wrong, you'll get best results by discussing the problem with the job supervisor.

Permits and Approvals

Building codes are written to set the minimum property standards for your area. Most areas rely on a combination of national, state, and local laws; others rely strictly on national codes. Code enforcement in your area depends on how much control the city or county wants over building within the community. National codes change very seldom, but local ones change frequently.

Building codes are designed to protect public safety. They are for the benefit of the person having the construction work done and for future buyers.

Some people believe that building codes exist only to fill city or county coffers by increasing the tax base on the house. Some people even try to conceal home-improvement projects to avoid an increase in taxes. They will eventually get caught when the house is sold and goes through escrow and the transfer of title—or, tragically, if there is a fire that can be traced to a faulty electrical item

that was not installed according to code and was never approved. If this can be proved, their fire insurance may be voided.

Most building inspectors deal not with inexperienced homeowners but with professional builders and architects who know exactly what is required to apply for and obtain a permit. In order to prevent problems that may arise, find out exactly what is needed to obtain a permit. Many building departments offer a free booklet outlining what is required for that city or county.

In most cases, the application for a building permit must include information about the type and scope of the construction. It usually also includes the approximate starting date and cost of the project, as well as the names and addresses of the general contractor and all subcontractors.

You must submit a detailed plan view drawing of your spa, indicating where all of the components will be installed and where the electrical, water, and gas hookups will be located. You must include all relevant sizes, shapes, dimensions, and structural details of all items, and the distances from the items to all property lines. In most cases you will need only two permits—a building permit and an electrical permit.

The building inspector will be checking your plans against laws governing the environment, zoning, height, set-back,

and easement restrictions. These laws are designed to protect the neighborhood in order to maintain its character and to assure adequate fire and utility access.

Take the completed plans to the building department and talk with one of the inspectors. You will usually need to submit a minimum of two sets of plans. Some building departments have special after-hours days, when busy homeowners can come in and discuss their plans after the department's normal business hours. If the staff members are not too busy at this time, they may look over the plans, locate any possible problems, and make suggestions. If there is a problem, discuss it with them and see if a variance is possible for that specific problem. You may need to ask the planning commission or city council for a variance. Building inspectors are employed to enforce the building code; don't try to make them bend the rules for your particular job.

After your plans are final and the permit is issued, the department will inform you of the different stages of construction to be inspected and approved. The permit must be displayed on the job site so the inspector can sign off on the different stages. When you are ready for an inspection, call the building department and make an appointment for an inspector to come out to the job site. If there is a problem with one stage of the work, it must be corrected and approved before proceeding to the next stage.

Nature may have provided the perfect spa location with an imperfect slope. This problem can be solved, however. The solutions range from hand leveling to building extensive retaining walls. The solution can even become a creative addition to the landscaping around the spa.

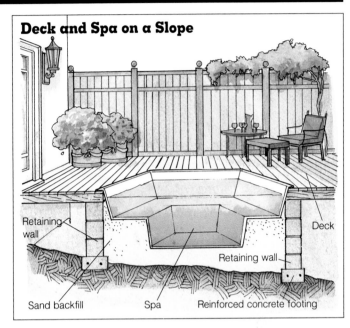

Deck and Spa on a Slope

Retaining wall

Deck

Retaining wall

Sand backfill

Spa

Reinforced concrete footing

Site Grading and Excavation

The ground surface around the spa must be level to provide a solid base for any decks that will surround the spa. A reasonably flat surface can be leveled by hand. If extensive excavation is required, you should consider having this work done by an excavation contractor. This is also true if a retaining wall must be added or if numerous footings must be installed. A qualified contractor will usually get the job done better and more quickly than you could, and in most cases the cost of hiring an excavation contractor is money well spent.

Excavation for a Sunken Indoor Spa

If the spa is to be partially or completely installed in the floor, the floor must be opened up and the ground below excavated to make room for the spa. Be sure you have an approved building permit before you proceed with this type of major structural change to your house.

If the house has a concrete slab floor, the floor opening should be cut by a contractor with a concrete coring machine. After all of the cuts are completed, the slab must be broken up and removed. The thickness of the concrete floor will determine how the floor can be broken up for removal. You may be able to use sledge hammers or, if the floor is too thick, you may need a pneumatic jackhammer. These are available from tool rental outlets.

If the house has a wood-frame floor, the floor can be cut away with a saw and then removed. The immediate area must be temporarily reinforced to carry the weight of the surrounding unsupported floor structure. The final floor reinforcement is usually done after the dirt is removed from under the floor. This new reinforcement must also support the weight of the new spa.

After the floor surface is removed, excavation of the ground below is basically the same as for an outdoor spa. However, there may not be room inside the house for power digging equipment. You will also need a pathway to carry out the debris and soil that result from opening up the floor and digging the hole.

Excavation for an Outdoor Spa

If the spa is to be partially or completely installed in the ground, the area must be excavated. You will need a hole for the spa and a trench or trenches for water and utility lines. The trenches extend from the spa to the support-equipment location and from there to the main hookup at the house or out to the street. If your plan includes outdoor lighting, trenches for this wiring should be dug at the same time.

If the spa is to be set completely into the ground, the excavation will be extensive and will result in a very large pile of dirt. To save the cost of hauling off the removed dirt, you may decide to use it elsewhere in the yard as fill or to create a raised berm for grass or plantings.

The hole must be large enough to accommodate the spa, its external plumbing, and wet-sand backfilling. If you are installing a small to medium-sized spa, the hole can be dug with a pick and shovel—if you don't mind the hard work. If the spa is large or you don't want to perform this type of manual labor, you can hire an excavating company. With the proper equipment, an excavator can do the job in a day or two, depending on spa size.

Before you start digging the hole and trenches, check again to make sure there are no underground utilities, sewer lines, or water pipes in the areas where you will be digging.

The top rim of the spa should be higher than any ground surface around it. Even if the spa is to be surrounded by a deck, it must be elevated above the surrounding ground to keep deck water runoff from draining into the spa.

Establish the level of the top rim of the spa in relation to the existing ground surface. For example, if the spa is 5 feet deep but the final installed rim height will be 1½ feet above the ground, dig a hole about 4 feet deep. This allows ½ foot for backfilling with wet sand. You should allow 4 to 6 inches of extra depth and 10 to 16 inches of extra width around the entire spa for sand backfilling.

After you have established the orientation of the spa in the yard, make an outline of the spa, plus the additional 10 to 16 inches for clearance, on the ground with stakes and string or gypsum powder. Once the outline is established, the locations of the different levels for the footwells and seats must be established. The positions and depth of all of these locations is very important, since you don't want a hole that is too small or too large. Take your time and dig the hole with the vertical and horizontal clearances previously described. Be sure to allow room for the plumbing, drains, and any electrical fixtures. Make sure there is also room for the bottom drain if the spa is equipped with one.

The bottom surface of the excavation should be firm soil, preferably undisturbed residual soil that has been compacted over the years. This will provide a firm base for the spa. Do not dig too deep into the bottom surface, or you will have to backfill with less stable transported soil. If the undisturbed residual soil is sandy or unstable, you may want to consider pouring a concrete slab in the base to provide a good footing for the spa. This surface, not the backfilling of sand, establishes the solid base for the spa.

Construction of Retaining Walls

If the ground surface for the spa site is on a slope, the ground must be graded until it is level. This usually involves a cut-and-fill procedure in which the high ground is cut and

moved to the lower ground to fill it in. You will usually need a retaining wall on the lower side to hold the newly moved dirt in place. If the original grade of the site was quite severe, it may be necessary to install a retaining wall at the higher side as well.

Retaining walls can be made from poured concrete, concrete block, reinforced bricks, large rocks, and so on. These walls can be turned into a real asset in the landscaping of the yard, because they create different levels to use in interesting ways, such as for plantings or seating. The retaining wall is placed on a concrete footing. In some cases reinforcement bars are required for stability. Check your local building code since requirements vary considerably in different areas.

Retaining Walls for an Aboveground Built-in Spa

A built-in spa can be installed aboveground simply by building retaining walls to surround and support the spa on all sides. The retaining walls must be built tall enough to encompass the spa depth. The spa site doesn't have to be level, but the finished top surface of the retaining walls must be level in all directions so the spa will be level when it is installed. This is necessary for proper drainage.

If you are handy with concrete-block walls and don't want to get involved in extensive excavation, this is an alternate way to install your spa. Actually, retaining walls can be made from a number of different materials—for example, stone, brick, pressure-treated

timber—as long as they are strong enough to support a spa filled with water and people. Exposed walls can be covered with the same type of wood used on any decks.

The only excavation required for this type of installation is a ditch under the wall foundation for the water pipes and utility lines to pass through.

Site Preparation for Portable Spas

A portable spa can be placed on various types of ground support materials. Some portable spas are completely enclosed on the bottom and can be placed on almost any surface.

Aboveground Portable Spas

The ground surface used for a portable spa must be level in all directions so that when the spa is placed on top of it, the spa will be level. This is necessary for proper drainage. See the section on site excavation (page 12) for surface preparation to obtain a level spa site. After the ground is level it can be covered with pea gravel, bricks, precast concrete stepping stones, wooden decking, or a poured concrete pad.

A concrete pad is relatively easy to build. It can follow the outline of the spa, or it can be made larger to surround the spa. The form can be fabricated from 2 by 4s, using wooden stakes to hold the form in place. Using 2 by 4s for the form will result in a concrete pad that is about 3½ inches thick.

Remove 2 to 3 inches of dirt from the entire area within the form below the bottom surface. Fill in this area to the bottom of

the form with clean sand or pea gravel and level it off. On top of the sand or pea gravel, make a latticework of ½-inch reinforcing bars (rebars), laid in a grid of 1-foot squares. Place a layer of rebars in one direction 12 inches apart, then place a second layer, also 12 inches apart, at right angles to the first. Where the rebars intersect, tie them together with wire. This will form a grid that adds rigidity to the concrete pad.

Fill in the form with concrete and level it off with a wood screed. After the form is completely filled and leveled, finish the surface using a float and finishing trowel. If the edges will be visible, finish them with an edging tool. Allow the concrete to cure for two to three days before placing the spa on it.

In-Ground Portable Spas

A portable spa can be installed in the ground so the top surface of the spa is level with the surrounding spa site or decking. To do this, a pit must be excavated, and a foundation, retaining walls, and concrete floor complete with drain, must be installed. This is a lot of work, but it will enable you to install a totally insulated spa in the ground. If the spa is installed in this manner, you must leave a space between the side of the spa and the wall of the pit. Check your local building code for the distance required in your area.

If a deck is installed around the spa, there should be a hinged door in the decking to allow access to the support equipment.

INSTALLING SPA FITTINGS

For the ultimate do-it-yourselfer, installing the spa fittings may provide the satisfaction of having done every possible step of the job. For the less determined, it may make more sense to buy a spa that is already equipped with all the necessary plumbing.

Advantages and Disadvantages

Most spas come with fittings such as the skimmer and hydrojets already installed. If you prefer to do every possible step when installing a spa, one option is to purchase the bare spa shell, cut all of the holes, and install all of the plumbing and electrical fittings yourself. A bare shell can be purchased from some spa manufacturers. A word of caution: If you install all the hardware yourself, the manufacturer may not guarantee the spa. Spa manufacturers want to install all items according to their quality assurance standards and then test them at the factory. If they allow you to install the fittings, they no longer have control over the quality. Another thing to remember is that if an electric drill, hole saw, or hand tool slips, you may ruin the finished surface of a perfectly good spa shell. If the damage is severe, you may have to purchase a new shell or live with the mistake.

General Guidelines

If you choose to install the fittings yourself, follow these tips to avoid problems. Component designs vary, so be sure to follow any special instructions shipped with separate fittings.

• Set the spa shell on the ground. Block it securely so it will not shift or move around when you are drilling or cutting holes. Make sure you have sufficient working space on all sides.
• Use only sharp drill bits or hole saws. Drill all holes from the inner finished surface of the spa shell toward the outer surface. When a drill bit or hole saw exits the opposite side, the spa-shell surface may chip or fracture. This presents no problem on the outer surface, since it will not be seen, but if it occurs on the inner surface there may be visible damage.
• Before drilling a hole, thoroughly check the outer side of the spa shell to make sure you will not be drilling into an air channel or reinforcement rib.
• To prevent water leaks, apply silicone sealant to all fitting gaskets. Don't use too much silicone sealant, though, especially on the inner surface, as this sealant must be cleaned off later.
• For a drill and cutout template for irregularly shaped holes, use the gasket or faceplate—that is, the trim plate installed on the inner surface of the spa. Correctly position the gasket on the spa shell and draw the outline and hole locations on the shell with a grease pencil or fine-line permanent marking pen. Don't make the marks too heavy, because they may show after the fixture is installed.
• Install all plumbing fittings and pipe as close to the spa shell as possible. This will keep the size of the excavation to a minimum. It will also reduce the possibility of added stress on the fixtures and spa shell if the plumbing sticks out too far and is hit accidentally during installation.
• If tee fittings are used in water or air lines, install them with the open end down to prevent debris from falling into the fittings before the plumbing system is completed.
• When laying PVC pipe in the trench from the spa to the support equipment, always position it with the identification strip facing up so the building inspector can read it. This mark identifies the type and grade of pipe and will also indicate whether it is certified for use with natural gas.

Hydrojets

The plumbing layout and the size of the water and air pipes vary according to the number of jets to be installed in the spa. The water lines are usually 1½-inch PVC, and the air lines vary from ½ to 1½ inches, depending on the manufacturer of the hydrojet.

The number and placement of the hydrojets is largely a matter of personal preference. However, the number of jets may also be determined by the size of the pump you are going to use since a small pump will not provide enough force for a lot of hydrojets, and a large pump could put stress on a small number of hydrojets. It is a good idea to look at the standard location of the jets on the same model spa as yours, since the manufacturer went to a lot of trouble deciding where the jets should be placed for maximum use and comfort.

Choose the locations for the hydrojets and mark them on

Although installing fittings in a bare spa shell is not a complicated procedure, it usually isn't worth the extra effort.

the inner wall of the spa shell. Use a sharp drill bit and hole saw and drill the hole from the inner surface of the spa shell toward the outer surface.

Place the hydrojet in the hole, following the manufacturer's instructions. Apply a coat of silicone sealant to the gasket surface that faces the spa shell. Don't apply sealant to both sides or the gasket will be forced out of alignment when the fittings are tightened securely. The gasket must stay centered on the hole to prevent water leakage.

After you tighten the fittings, allow the silicone sealant to cure completely, then carefully trim away any excess sealant from the inner surface of the spa. It is unnecessary to remove any excess from the outer surface.

After all the hydrojets are installed and the silicone sealant is completely cured, the water and air pipes can be attached. If the sides of the spa are flat, rigid PVC pipe can be used; if the sides are curved, flexible PVC pipe should be installed. Using rigid PVC pipe on a spa with curved surfaces will place unnecessary strain on the hydrojet fittings and could cause leaks or fractures in the pipe or the fittings. Installation methods for the two types of pipe differ; refer to PVC Plumbing Techniques in this chapter (page 84) for details.

The hydrojets should be connected to a water-line system so the heated water enters the spa consistently on all sides. If there are eight hydrojets in the spa, four should be on one side of the system and four on the other, with the water coming from the water pump and heater entering at the center and being evenly distributed to both sides.

After the water pipes are connected, the air pipes must be attached to the hydrojets. The same type of PVC pipe used for the water connections should also be used for the air connections. The air pipes should be laid out as the water pipes were, so the air enters the spa at the center and is evenly distributed to both sides. The air jets can be connected to the air pipe with one valve that controls the air coming out of all hydrojets at the same velocity, or a control can be installed for each hydrojet so each one can be adjusted individually. Individual controls are usually mounted on the spa lip directly above the hydrojet.

Skimmer

The bottom edge of the inside opening of the skimmer should be level with the waterline in the spa.

Position the faceplate on the inner surface of the spa shell and lightly draw the outline and hole locations on the shell with a grease pencil or fine-line permanent marking pen. Don't make the marks too big because they may show after the fixture is installed.

Using a sharp bit, drill the mounting holes first. After the mounting holes are drilled, cut out the main opening. Drill a pilot hole in the center of the main opening with a drill large enough to accept a saber-saw blade. Cover the foot of the saber saw with masking tape or duct tape to prevent it from scratching the spa-shell surface.

Use a fine-tooth blade to prevent chipping the shell surface. Carefully and slowly cut out the main opening with the saber saw. If necessary, use a fine-cut file and smooth the edge created by the saber saw. Insert the skimmer into the spa shell and see if it fits correctly. You may have to file away some additional material for the final fit.

If the spa shell has polyurethane foam insulation sprayed on the outer surface, this must be removed from the area where the skimmer will be installed. The surface must be smooth, as it is the sealing side for the skimmer. Chip off the insulation and buff the surface with sandpaper, then wipe off the surface so there is no dirt or dust on it.

Apply silicone sealant to both sides of the gasket, unless directed otherwise by the manufacturer's instructions, and install the skimmer. After the mounting hardware is attached and tightened, apply additional silicone sealant to the backs of the fasteners to eliminate any possible water leaks.

Allow the sealant to cure completely, then carefully trim away any excess sealant from the inner surface of the spa. It is not necessary to remove excess from the outer surface.

Air Blower

The blower is very easy to install and is usually connected to the spa with flexible 2-inch PVC pipe.

It's important to protect the air blower from any backflow of water into the motor. This problem can be prevented by installing a check valve or by constructing a raised loop in the air line.

If the air-blower motor is quite a distance from the spa, water can flow back into the air pipe. This places a strain on the motor by requiring it to push the water back out of the line. Air-blower motors are not designed to move water—only air. Also, during cold winter months any water trapped in the pipe could freeze, expand, and break the pipe.

Install a check valve or raised loop in the air-blower pipe as close to the spa inlet as possible, since this will minimize the amount of water that could flow into the pipe. A check valve is easier to install but is also more expensive than a raised loop. A check valve allows air or water to move in only one direction through the pipe. The raised loop, constructed of rigid PVC pipe, is connected to the air-blower inlet fitting on the spa, then rises above the top lip of the spa and drops down to the air-blower pipe that extends to the air-blower motor.

Drains

Depending on building codes in your area, the spa may be required to have either a single or double drain. Usually there is a main drain in the base or the lowest section of the spa. Some codes also require an additional side drain. The second drain reduces the suction force of the water as it leaves the spa. Where two drains are required, they are usually placed about 12 inches apart. To prevent a whirlpool effect as the water drains, an antivortex cover may be required.

PRETESTING THE SPA

Before lowering the spa into the ground or taking it into the house, it's a good idea to pretest it for water leaks or lighting-system problems. This is especially important if you installed the fittings in a bare spa shell yourself. These problems will be easier to repair while the outside of the spa shell is still conveniently accessible.

Tests for Water Leaks

Test all the plumbing piping, fixtures, and fittings for leaks. If you installed the fittings yourself, the test should be performed after the silicone sealant used on the plumbing fittings has had a chance to cure. Wait 2 to 3 hours before filling the spa with water.

Some spas come with a wooden support structure already attached to the spa shell for installation. If the spa is not equipped with this structure, use wooden blocks to securely support the perimeter of the spa and the seating and floor areas so the spa will not shift or move while it is being filled with water. If the spa is equipped with a bottom drain, dig a hole to make room for it so it will not be damaged.

The inlet and outlet pipes or fittings on the spa must be capped with temporary expandable plugs designed for this purpose. These plugs are intended to be installed and removed—don't use sealant or cement to hold them in place. If you are unable to buy the plugs locally, temporarily connect a piece of flexible PVC pipe to each fitting and run the loose ends of the pipe above the spa waterline. Use duct tape to secure the loose ends to the side of the spa or to a stepladder placed alongside the spa.

Remove the protective plastic wrap or cardboard from the spa shell. Carefully remove any dirt or debris from the interior of the spa, then slowly fill the spa with cold water from a garden hose. Don't go away to do something else while the spa is filling; stay there. If you leave, Murphy's law guarantees that a support will shift or slip, and the spa may end up on its side with water running out, possibly even filling up the excavation.

As the spa fills with water, continuously check for leaks at the lower fittings and fixtures. If you notice a leak, turn the water off immediately. Drain the water below the level of the leak and investigate the problem. Leaks may be caused by damaged fittings, insufficient sealer where the fittings are installed on the spa shell, or poorly made pipe joints. If the leak is caused by a manufacturer's error, discuss repairs with the spa dealer. Don't try to patch a leak with sealer; remove the component or disconnect the joint, then redo the installation or pipe connection. After the problem is fixed,

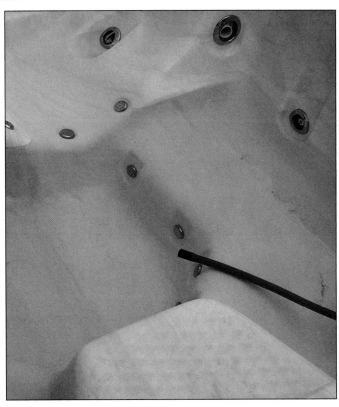
The spa should be checked for leaks before it is installed.

continue filling the spa and check for additional leaks. Fill the spa until the water reaches the bottom of the skimmer outlet. Allow the spa to remain filled with water for at least half a day and make sure there are no leaks. If you have a leak that you cannot fix yourself, contact the spa dealer or spa installer for their assistance in solving the problem.

If you are satisfied that there are no water leaks, drain the spa. If you don't want to drain the water in the immediate area, use a swimming pool drain hose. If the plug has been installed, remove it from the drain and temporarily attach a swimming pool drain hose

onto the fitting, or slip the loose end of the flexible PVC hose into a long length of swimming pool drain hose. Place the other end of the drain hose in the desired area away from the work site and drain the spa. If necessary, repeat this procedure for the other hose, then carefully tip the spa to one side to empty as much water as possible. Be sure not to damage any of the plumbing pipes or fittings while tipping the spa.

Tests for Lights

If the spa is equipped with interior lights, check them at this time. Temporarily connect the lights to the correct voltage source (12 volts or 110 volts) and make sure they work properly. Repair any problem before installing the spa.

INSTALLING PLUMBING

Plumbing is a time-consuming part of installing a spa, but you can achieve substantial savings by doing it yourself. With the tools listed at the beginning of this chapter and a good supply of patience, you should be able to plumb the spa without problems.

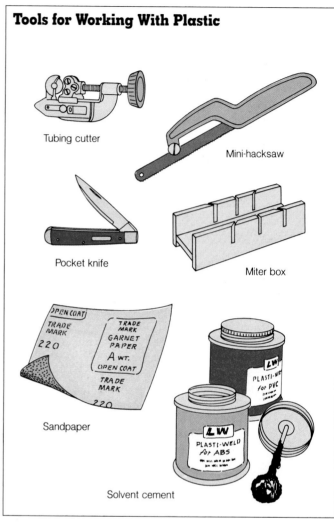

Tools for Working With Plastic

Tubing cutter

Mini-hacksaw

Pocket knife

Miter box

Sandpaper

Solvent cement

PVC Plumbing Techniques

Plumbing the spa with PVC pipe and fittings is usually acceptable. PVC pipe is either rigid or flexible, and most fittings are of the slip-joint type. Before buying PVC pipe and fittings, consult your local building code to make sure PVC pipe is permitted in your area for spa installations. If PVC pipe is acceptable, find out what the pipe diameter and wall thickness requirements are. PVC pipe is manufactured in various wall thicknesses and grades for different applications.

All PVC plumbing components are manufactured to the same basic specifications, but there are slight variations between different manufacturers, so try to purchase all of your plumbing supplies from one company in order to ensure a proper fit. The fittings usually have the manufacturer's name or logo printed on them.

If you can't get all of the necessary components from the same manufacturer, use this simple test to make sure the fittings and pipe are compatible. Take a short section of the PVC pipe that you will be using and install the pipe into the fittings from the other manufacturer. The pipe should enter the fitting and meet some resistance partway in. Hold onto

the pipe and let the fitting hang down from it. The fitting should stay on the pipe. If the fitting falls off, it should not be used, as it will not provide a watertight joint.

The solvent cement and cleaner/primer must be matched exactly to the type of pipe that is being joined. There are four specific types of solvent cement and one all-purpose kind. Be sure to purchase the correct one for rigid PVC pipe. If you use flexible PVC pipe, you must use a solvent cement formulated specifically for this type of pipe. Do not use cement intended for rigid PVC pipe; you will not get a watertight connection. The labels on most solvent-cement cans specify the type of pipe for which the cement is formulated.

A word of caution: The solvent cement and cleaner/primer vapors are harmful to breathe and are also flammable. *Avoid prolonged breathing of the vapors, and install the cap and dauber on the can after each use.* This not only reduces the harmful fumes but keeps the solution from drying out.

Solvent welding of the pipe to the fittings is a one-way street. You can put the two pieces together, but you cannot separate them. If you make a

mistake by installing the wrong fitting, you must cut the pipe and remove it, then use special couplings to install the correct fitting into the system. Don't try to pull the fitting off the pipe because the solvent cement actually melts both components to form a complete bond. Even if you can separate the two components they will be useless, since some of the material will transfer from one to the other. Most PVC fittings are of the slip-joint type, which requires the use of solvent cement. Some PVC fittings are threaded and require silicone sealant on the threads to achieve a watertight joint.

Rigid PVC Pipe

To work with rigid PVC pipe, you will need a PVC pipe cutter or a fine-tooth backsaw or hacksaw with a minimum of 24 teeth per inch. A fine-tooth blade is necessary in order to get a clean cut. You should also have a miter box to hold the pipe in order to get a square cut. A square cut is essential to join the pipe correctly with its fitting.

After the pipe is cut, use a knife and clean off all burrs and slightly bevel the outer end of the pipe. This will make it easy to insert the pipe into the fitting. The inner surface of

Cutting and Joining Plastic Pipe

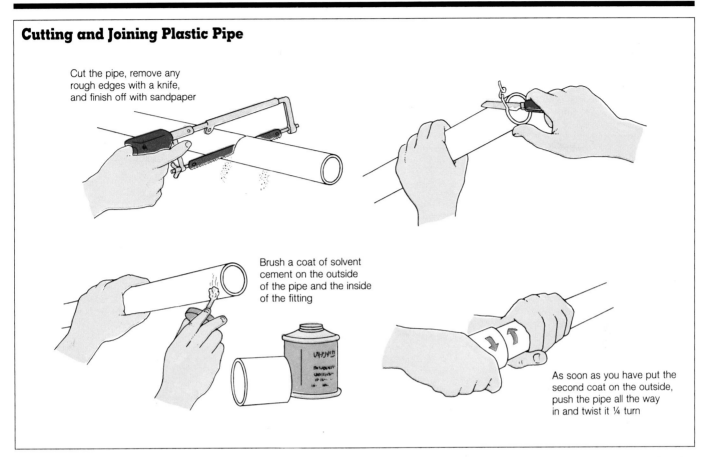

Cut the pipe, remove any
rough edges with a knife,
and finish off with sandpaper

Brush a coat of solvent
cement on the outside
of the pipe and the inside
of the fitting

As soon as you have put the
second coat on the outside,
push the pipe all the way
in and twist it ¼ turn

the fitting and the outer surface of the pipe must be free of dirt and grease. Wipe each piece with a clean cloth.

Most solvent cement is highly flammable, so do not allow anyone to smoke in the area while you are using the solvent cement. Don't work next to an open flame or pilot light on a household appliance.

The dauber or brush attached to the cleaner/primer and solvent-cement cap should be at least one third to one half the size of the pipe diameter. This is necessary to apply the correct amount of solvent cement to both parts.

Apply the cleaner/primer to both the fitting socket and the outer surface of the pipe. Apply the cleaner/primer about 1 inch past the fitting-connection area on the pipe. By doing

this the cleaner/primer will be visible when the spa plumbing is examined by the building inspector.

After the solvent cement is applied to the pipe and fitting, the two pieces must be joined immediately and rotated about ¼ turn. This will then be the orientation of the fitting to the pipe. For this reason, you must correctly position the fitting onto the pipe so it will align correctly with the next piece of pipe after being rotated. Be sure to figure this out before applying the solvent cement and putting the pieces together.

Apply a liberal coat of solvent cement to the pipe and a lighter coat to the fitting socket. If you apply too much to the

fitting socket, the pipe will push it into the fitting and restrict the opening. Immediately push the fitting onto the pipe and rotate it in the desired direction about 90 degrees. The solvent cement should still be wet at this time. Hold the fitting on the pipe in this position for about 1 minute to allow the cement to set up. As the fitting is pushed onto the pipe, some of the solvent cement will bunch up on the end of the fitting and form a fillet of cement and dissolved plastic— don't remove this; it is part of the watertight seal.

Flexible PVC Pipe

The flexible type of PVC pipe requires its own special solvent cement. The pipe should be cut with a very sharp knife; do not

try to cut it with a backsaw or hacksaw as you will end up with a ragged cut, making it difficult to attach the flexible pipe to its fittings.

Use medium-grit sandpaper to roughen the surface of the flexible PVC pipe slightly so it bonds securely to the fitting. Apply the special PVC solvent cement just as you would in using rigid PVC pipe. When you install flexible PVC pipe into a fitting, push and gently turn the flexible pipe in a counterclockwise direction (as seen from the end of the fitting). If you turn the pipe in the opposite direction, the coil construction of the pipe will expand and will not allow the pipe to enter the fitting completely; the resulting improper joint will leak water. Hold the fitting on the pipe in this position for about 5 to 10 minutes to allow the cement to set up. As the fitting is pushed onto the pipe, some of the solvent cement will bunch up on the end of the fitting and form a fillet of cement and plastic; don't remove it, as this helps form a watertight seal. The size of the fillet is considerably less than with rigid PVC pipe.

Copper Plumbing Techniques

There are two basic types of copper pipe or tubing—rigid and flexible. Flexible pipe is usually used for home repairs, whereas rigid pipe is used for new home construction and can be used for the spa water system. Spas are usually plumbed with PVC pipe, but in some spas copper pipe must be used, either exclusively or in conjunction with PVC.

Copper pipe is available in three different wall thicknesses. Thin-wall pipe is Type M; medium-wall pipe is Type L; and thick-wall pipe is Type K. The greater the wall thickness, the more the pipe costs per foot. In most cases, Type L (medium wall) is acceptable for home construction and spa installations, but check your local building code to be sure which type and diameter of copper pipe is required in your area.

There are various kinds of fittings that mate copper to copper, and copper to PVC or cast-iron pipe. Fittings used to mate copper pipe to threaded pipe must be made of brass. When a transition is made from copper to plastic (PVC), you must use a plastic female (inner threads) to a metallic male (outer threads) or an approved stainless-steel mechanical-compression coupling that employs a synthetic rubber elastomeric sealing sleeve. This type of compression fitting must be restrained from movement. These fittings are usually available from hardware stores or the supplier of the copper pipe. Look at their selections so you know what is available and in what sizes. When you buy fittings, be sure they are compatible with the size of pipe you are using. Copper pipe comes in nominal sizes of ¼ inch, ⅜ inch, ½ inch, and so on, and in diameters up to 2 inches.

Copper pipe is best cut with a tubing cutter, but you can use a fine-tooth hacksaw with a minimum of 24 teeth per inch. Tubing cutters are inexpensive and produce smooth, square cuts. A square cut is essential to join the pipe securely to its fittings. If you use a hacksaw, you should also use a miter box to hold the pipe while cutting it in order to get a square cut.

When measuring the length of pipe that will be positioned between two fittings that are already installed, take into consideration the amount of pipe that will slide into each fitting. This dimension is usually about ½ inch per fitting. Copper pipe is expensive, so you don't want to waste any by ending up with short lengths of pipe that can't be used.

After the pipe is cut it must be cleaned of any burrs. Use a flat, fine-cut file to smooth all burrs from the outer surface of the pipe. Clean all burrs from

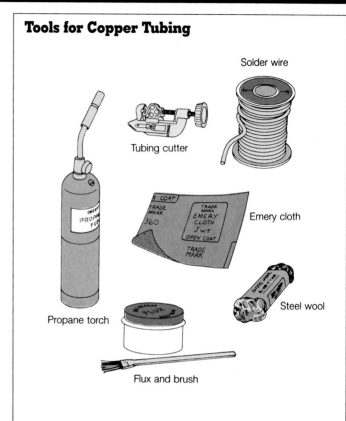

Tools for Copper Tubing

Solder wire

Tubing cutter

Emery cloth

Steel wool

Propane torch

Flux and brush

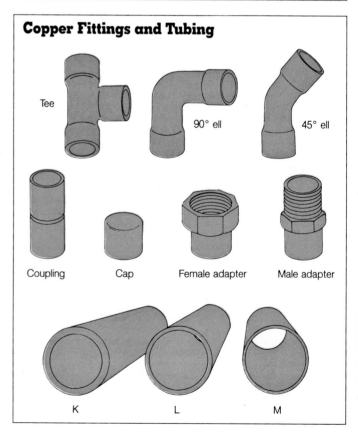

Copper Fittings and Tubing

Tee

90° ell

45° ell

Coupling

Cap

Female adapter

Male adapter

K

L

M

Sweating Copper Tubing

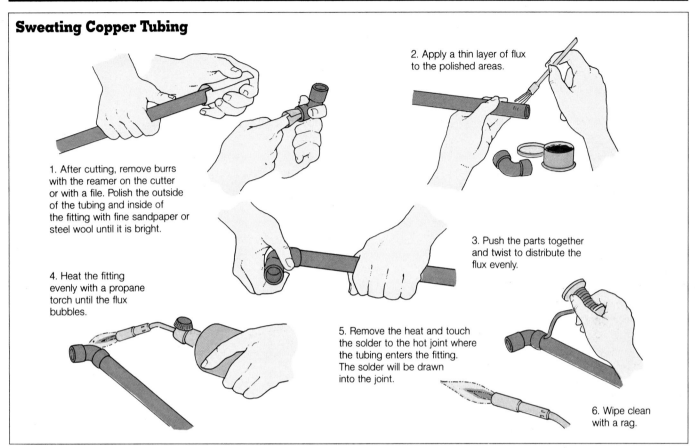

1. After cutting, remove burrs with the reamer on the cutter or with a file. Polish the outside of the tubing and inside of the fitting with fine sandpaper or steel wool until it is bright.

2. Apply a thin layer of flux to the polished areas.

3. Push the parts together and twist to distribute the flux evenly.

4. Heat the fitting evenly with a propane torch until the flux bubbles.

5. Remove the heat and touch the solder to the hot joint where the tubing enters the fitting. The solder will be drawn into the joint.

6. Wipe clean with a rag.

the inner surface of the pipe with the reamer that is usually built into tubing cutters, or with a half-round or rat-tail file. This will make it easy to insert the pipe into the fitting and will eliminate any internal restrictions.

The method of attaching copper fittings to copper pipe is called "sweat soldering." To achieve a leakproof sweat-soldered joint, make sure the joint is tight from the very beginning. Resoldering a joint that has leaked is very difficult since all water must be evacuated from the line before making the repair. You will need a propane torch, noncorrosive solder paste or flux, and a solid-core solder for this procedure.

Copper pipe and fittings tend to oxidize when they sit for long on a shelf in a hardware store. This oxidation, and any dirt or grease, must be removed before doing any soldering. Buff the outer surface of the pipe and the inner surface of the fitting with fine sandpaper or steel wool. After buffing, wipe each piece with a clean cloth to remove all debris.

After the pipe and fittings are thoroughly cleaned, apply a layer of solder paste or flux to the outer surface of the pipe and the inner surface of the fitting socket. Apply the solder paste or flux with a flux brush or an old toothbrush. Make sure all surfaces are completely covered; this prevents the copper from oxidizing when heated with a propane torch.

After the pipe and fitting are coated with the solder paste or flux, install the fitting onto the pipe and position it in its correct orientation to the pipe. This fitting may have to match up with another piece of pipe or another fitting; if this alignment is critical, scratch an alignment line on the fitting and pipe with a scribe or nail so it can be seen during the soldering operation.

If you will be soldering in a confined area, place a heat-resistant panel behind the pipe and fitting to protect any object or surface behind them from the heat. Wear eye protection, since the solder paste or flux may sizzle out from the joint when the heat is applied.

With the fitting in place on the pipe, heat both pieces with

the propane torch. When the pipe and fitting are heated, the solder paste or flux will get hot and emit a vapor—do not breathe this vapor, as it may be caustic. Move the torch around the pipe so all sides are heated evenly. Uneven heat will cause the joint to leak water. Continue to heat the pipe and fitting until they are warm enough to melt the solder. To test this, touch the end of a piece of solder to the exterior of the fitting and see if it starts to melt.

It is important to remember that the pipe and fitting must be hot enough to melt the solder so that it will flow evenly between the two parts. Never melt the solder with the propane torch. When the joint is properly heated, the solder flux inside will draw the molten solder into the fitting to seal the connection.

When the two parts are hot enough to melt the solder, continue to heat the pipe with the torch ½ inch to 1 inch away from the fitting. Touch the solder to the end of the fitting and allow the solder to flow into the space between the fitting and the pipe. Continue to feed the solder into the joint until it appears to have filled the entire fissure around the fitting. If alignment marks were used, make sure they are still aligned; reposition the pipe and fitting with a tool if necessary. Remove the torch and immediately wipe off any excess solder with a heavy cloth, taking care not to disturb the fitting while doing this. Allow the pipe and fitting to cool naturally—don't wet them to shorten the cool-off period.

After the pipe has cooled, an additional joint can then be soldered. When performing the second soldering operation, you must prevent the first soldered joint from getting hot, because the solder may melt and the fitting may slide off or rotate out of position. To prevent this, soak a towel in cold water and wrap it around the completed joint. This is usually sufficient to keep the solder from melting.

After all soldering is done, thoroughly wipe off all residual solder paste or flux from all joints and pipes, as it is usually caustic.

Insulating the Water Pipes

Spa water loses heat by a number of means. For built-in spas, one of these ways is through the water pipes that run from the spa to the support equipment. Long water pipes can cause a significant temperature loss, especially in cold climates where the ground never gets really warm.

After the water-pipe system is installed and checked for leakage, it can be insulated for energy conservation as well as for protection against freezing. Insulating the pipes may reduce by half the heat loss from the pipes. Foam sleeves and tape are available from spa dealers and hardware stores. These foam tubes were originally designed to insulate household water systems in cold climates.

Preformed sleeves slide over the PVC water lines, and special preformed pieces fit over PVC elbows and tee fittings. The foam pieces are then taped in place until the trench is backfilled with dirt. There is also a foam tape that can be used on fittings if no preformed pieces are available.

Hydrojet air lines can also be insulated with a special tape available from some spa dealers.

Connection of Natural Gas Lines

If the water heater of your spa uses natural gas, a natural-gas line hookup must be made from the house gas meter. There are many strict building code requirements pertaining to natural gas lines.

Consult your local building code for type and size requirements for natural gas pipe. Also

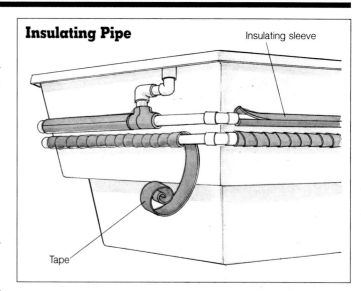

Insulating Pipe

Insulating sleeve

Tape

refer to the installation instructions furnished with the water heater. If there is a discrepancy between the requirements, check with the building department.

Most installations can use iron, steel (black or galvanized), yellow brass (containing no more than 75 percent copper), or PVC pipe that is formulated for use with natural gas. Pipe used for natural gas must be either new or, if it was previously used, it must have been used only for transporting natural gas and be in good condition. All fittings must be malleable iron, yellow brass (containing no more than 75 percent copper), or PVC approved for use with gas lines. All gas-line joints must be of the screw type with approved standard threads, and each joint sealed with an approved pipe-joint material that is insoluble in the presence of natural gas. The joint material is to be applied to the male threads (outer threads) only. No gas lines or fittings can have any type of strain put on them, nor can they be bent. The heater cannot be supported by the gas line,

as this would strain the line and possibly cause a leak.

The gas line must be buried in the ground to a specified depth to prevent accidental damage from digging in the yard. Usually PVC pipe has to be buried deeper than steel pipe; check with the building department for these specifications. If the run of the pipe is quite long, it is usually cheaper to use steel pipe so you will not have to dig the deeper trench.

Some building departments require that all gas pipes be sleeved—that is, passed through an outer line of larger diameter—and vented if they are going to be buried under concrete. No natural gas lines may be installed in or on the ground under a building or structure.

An approved shutoff valve must be installed in the gas line between the gas meter and the heater. The shutoff valve has to be located a specified distance from the heater, as stipulated in local building codes.

Many building departments also require that all fittings, connections, and risers be wrapped with a specified number of layers of gas-line tape to

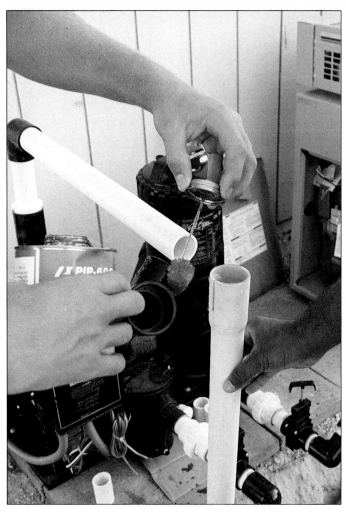

Apply primer and solvent cement to the inside of fittings and around the outside of the pipe. Use a scrap of cardboard to protect the area under the joint from drips, which are hard to remove.

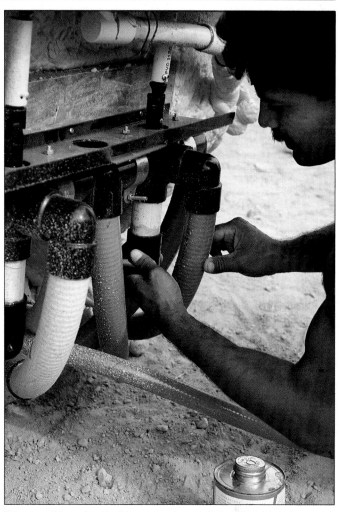

When possible, make plumbing connections and check for leaks before placing the spa in the ground, or at least before backfilling. The flexible and rigid pipes shown here require two different gluing techniques.

prevent corrosion and rust. In some cases the entire length of buried gas pipe and all risers must have a special protective wrapping due to soil conditions that may corrode the pipe.

If the special natural-gas PVC pipe is used, most codes require that the risers be steel to prevent breakage and a possible gas leak. Plumbing adapter fittings are available to make the change from PVC to steel pipe. Be sure to install the special natural-gas PVC pipe in the trench with the words "natural gas" facing up so the building inspector can see them. If PVC pipe is used, an

18-gauge metal tracer wire must be placed alongside the PVC pipe so it can be located with a metal detector later on. The tracer wire usually terminates aboveground at each end of the pipe.

After installation, the gas line must be pressure tested before being attached to the house gas meter or water heater. One end of the gas line must be capped and a special pump and pressure gauge attached to the other end. The gas line is then pumped up to a specific pressure; this pressure must be maintained for a specified period of time according to code requirements. Notify

the building department that you are ready for a rough gas inspection. After inspection, the special pump and gauge are disconnected. Attach a cap to this end of the gas line to prevent the entry of foreign material and leave it capped until it is connected to the house gas meter and water heater.

Connection of Other Fossil Fuels

If your spa water heater uses fuel oil, liquefied petroleum gas (LPG) or other types of fuel, the

fuel-line hookup must follow the codes for natural gas piping, with additional requirements as dictated by local building codes.

If LPG is used, the heater cannot be located in a pit or basement where the heavier-than-air LPG can accumulate and form a flammable vapor that could cause an explosion. All fittings must be joined with an approved pipe-joint material, applied to the male threads only, that is insoluble in the presence of LPG. PVC plastic pipe is not approved and cannot be used with LPG.

Electrical wiring brings the spa to life. The pumps and blowers that provide the soothing massage and the lighting that sets the mood depend on wiring. Although this work should be done by experts, you need to know what the experts will do.

Requirements for 110-V Spa Circuit

The portable spa comes wired with a 3-pronged, 15-foot grounded power cord. The 15-foot cord length is the maximum allowed by Underwriters' Laboratory; never attach this cord to an extension cord. This 15-foot cord must be plugged into a 20-ampere (amp) dedicated-circuit receptacle that is protected by a ground fault circuit interrupter (GFCI). A *dedicated circuit* means that this circuit and circuit breaker serve only the spa and nothing else—not even a light fixture.

Some spa manufacturers provide a 3-pronged, single-receptacle outlet that is compatible with the spa power cord. They may even provide a weather-resistant cover plate

This electrical panel includes an unused 220-volt circuit breaker for a future spa installation.

for the receptacle for outdoor installations. The National Electrical Code requires that the electrical outlet for the spa be installed no closer than 5 feet from the spa. In most cases the electrical outlet should also be no farther than 10 feet from the place where the power cord exits the compartment door on the spa skirting.

Have a licensed electrical contractor connect this electrical outlet to a 20-amp dedicated circuit. The orientation of the outlet should be matched to the power cord (that is, if the power cord ground terminal is at the bottom, the outlet ground terminal should also be at the bottom) so the power cord can hang straight down from the outlet. If you are installing the spa in an existing room, you may have to add a new 20-amp circuit for this installation.

Requirements for 220-V Spa Circuit

The electrical hookup of a 220-volt portable spa must be done correctly and according to local building code requirements. Have a licensed electrical contractor wire and complete all electrical hookups.

Some spa manufacturers provide a subpanel for the electrical hookup that is matched to the electrical requirements of that specific spa.

They may also include an electrical schematic of the recommended wiring and a wiring guide.

A 220-volt portable spa must be permanently wired and usually requires a 50-amp dedicated circuit. The electrical requirements for built-in spas vary because they all have different types of electrical support equipment. Usually this kind of installation requires a dedicated circuit and circuit breaker for each piece of electrical equipment.

Most building electrical codes require the installation of a ground fault circuit interrupter (GFCI) to protect any underwater spa lights and all electrical outlets within 15 feet of the spa. All exterior electrical boxes and fittings must be weatherproof, and electrical wires that traverse from the switch box or time clock to the main electrical panel must be in a waterproof conduit.

The additional circuit breakers for the spa should fit into the electrical main service panel of the house. If the existing main service panel is filled to capacity, another service subpanel must be installed to accommodate the extra electrical requirements of the spa. When adding a new service subpanel, install one that is large enough to handle not only the new spa requirements but also any future electrical needs. After the electrical circuits are connected to the circuit breakers, label each one according to which piece of support equipment it controls.

All electrical panels and subpanels must have front access. Electrical conduit that is

20-Amp Receptacle

run aboveground must be metal to avoid accidental severing of the conduit and wires. Electrical conduit run underground can be metal or specially formulated PVC that is labeled for electrical use. Electrical PVC is gray (PVC used for water systems is white). Be sure to install the special electrical PVC in the trench with its markings facing up so the building inspector can see them.

Like gas lines, electrical conduit must be buried to a certain depth in the ground to prevent accidental damage from digging in the yard. Usually, PVC has to be buried deeper than metal; consult the building code for these specifications.

All electrical components must be properly grounded or bonded according to local code requirements. In some cases the ground wire can be bonded to metal plumbing pipes (never use PVC pipe for grounding). In most instances, a grounding rod must be used as an electrical ground base. Check the building code for grounding requirements, including the necessary depth to which the grounding rod must be driven and the specified diameter of the rod. All support-equipment components are supplied with a ground lug for this purpose.

INSTALLING SUPPORT EQUIPMENT

The hard-working machinery that produces the warm, relaxing, bubbling environment of the spa should be out of sight and out of mind. Properly installed equipment, covered by a well-designed enclosure, will do its job without calling attention to itself.

Positioning Support Equipment

Support equipment for a built-in spa must be positioned to satisfy several requirements.

It should be located within 10 to 15 feet of the spa, a distance that allows the water pump and air blower to operate at maximum efficiency. This distance also minimizes heat loss from the water pipes.

The support equipment should be located on the same level as the spa, if possible. If the yard has a slope, the elevation difference must be taken into account when planning the installation.

The water-heater inlet should be on the same level as the spa; if it is not, the pressure switch of the heater must be recalibrated to compensate for the difference in elevation. Pressure-switch adjustment is fairly simple, and instructions for the task are usually included in the literature that accompanies the heater. If necessary, ask your spa dealer for instructions.

For the water pump to perform at maximum efficiency, it should be located below the spa water level to ensure that the pump is always self-primed for each start.

Since the assembly for the support equipment is not a thing of beauty, it is usually covered by an enclosure. If possible, select a location next to a wall or fence or on the side of the house so you can integrate the enclosure with one of these structures. The support equipment can also be installed in a garage, but there are specific requirements pertaining to this location, which are covered in this chapter on page 93.

If you are going to use air switches, a time clock, or exterior lighting, these controls can also be included in the support-equipment installation. After the site is selected, check the building code to make sure everything is located properly.

Mounting Support Equipment

All the mechanical and electrical support-equipment components must be placed on and attached to a concrete pad that is elevated from the surrounding ground surface.

Some home-improvement centers and large hardware stores carry precast concrete pads that are about 2 inches thick. If they are available, this is the easiest approach. If these precast pads are not available, you can easily pour a concrete pad yourself.

If you have purchased a skid pack (a package of support-equipment components), the manufacturer will usually provide size recommendations for the pad and instructions on how to attach the components.

If you purchased separate pieces of support equipment, connect the plumbing between all the pieces, as discussed in the following section. Once everything is connected, you will know how large a pad is required. Make sure the pad is big enough so the enclosure can also be attached to it. If you are going to pour a concrete pad, it's a good idea to design the enclosure at this time so you can include some attachment bolts in the concrete pad to secure the enclosure in place.

Make a raised flat-topped mound with sand on the ground where the concrete pad is to be poured or where the precast pads are to be placed. The pad must be elevated to prevent water from collecting around its base.

If you are going to pour a concrete pad, the form for the pad can be fabricated from 2 by 4s and wooden stakes to hold the forms in place. Place reinforcing mesh or a grid of #3 rebar within the forms two inches above the sand base.

Fill in the form with concrete and level it off with a wooden screed. After the form is completely filled and leveled, finish the surface with a float and steel finishing trowel. If any attachment bolts are to be added, place them in the concrete at this time and smooth out the concrete around the bolts. Allow the concrete to cure for 2 to 3 days before placing the support equipment on it. After the concrete has cured, attach the support equipment according to manufacturer's instructions.

Interconnecting Support Equipment

If you purchased separate pieces of support equipment, place all of the components on the ground in their correct relationship to each other. Use the information provided by the equipment manufacturers to position each unit. It is a good idea to actually connect the water pump, filter, and water heater with all of the correct pieces of plumbing pipe and fittings.

Unless a special draining system has been provided, it's advisable to add a hose bibb or gate valve between the water pump and filter to drain the spa for cleaning. A garden hose is used with the hose bibb; the PVC gate valve will accept a swimming pool drain hose for faster drainage.

To protect the filter from hot-water backflow, install a check valve between the filter and pump. These valves are available from spa dealers or large hardware stores.

Because of the high temperatures generated by the water heater, most manufacturers of fossil-fuel heaters require that a pipe made of metal (such as galvanized or stainless steel) be used on both the inlet and outlet sides of the heater for a specified distance. This is

Plumbing System

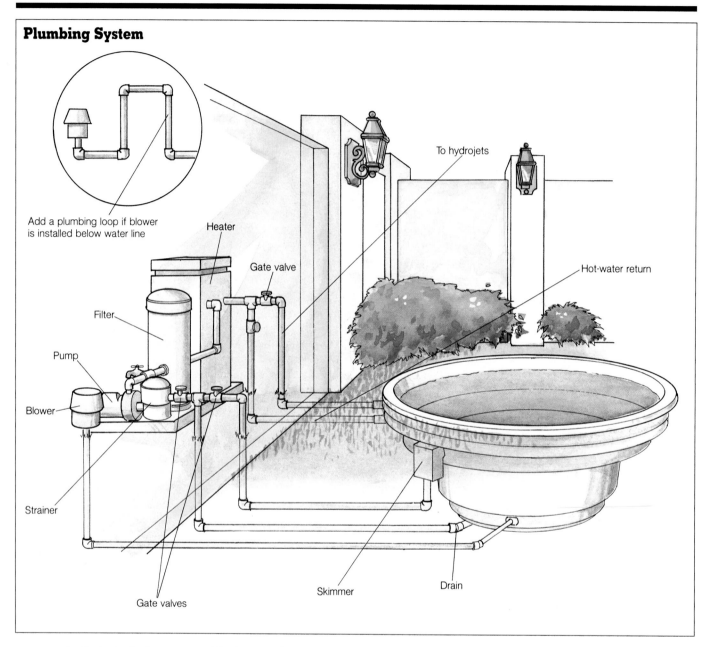

Add a plumbing loop if blower is installed below water line

Heater

Gate valve

To hydrojets

Hot-water return

Filter

Pump

Blower

Strainer

Gate valves

Skimmer

Drain

necessary to dissipate the heat generated by the heater. Adapters can be used to join the metal pipe to PVC pipe.

Be sure to install all pieces of plumbing that will be used with the support equipment. Connect the plumbing temporarily, without cement, to be sure everything fits together correctly. You may have to adjust the length of a piece of pipe to get a good fit or to

provide clearance for another piece of pipe. When the plumbing is attached temporarily and everything fits, make sure you have access to the electrical connections and to the gas-inlet fitting on the water heater. At this point, the pipe and fittings can be permanently connected to the support equipment, according to code, as described in

the next section. Except for the heater connections, all the plumbing connections can be made with rigid or flexible PVC pipe.

When working with threaded fittings, always wrap the male end of the fitting (external threads) with three or four layers of Teflon tape. Wrap the tape in a clockwise direction, as viewed when looking at the end of the

fitting, so the edge of the tape will not bunch up when the female portion of the fitting is screwed onto the male fitting. The use of Teflon tape is essential to achieve a watertight seal on this type of fitting. Always remove all of the old tape and replace it with new Teflon tape every time the fitting is disconnected. Always start threaded fittings by hand until resistance is felt, then use a wrench or slip-joint pliers to tighten them an additional full turn. Do not overtighten threaded fittings, as you may crack the female portion.

Attaching Support Equipment

There are many kinds of support-equipment connections. The plumbing layout is different between one-pump and two-pump systems; if swim jets are used, there is still another way to plumb the spa. If the spa manufacturer has provided instructions for the correct layout of the water and air lines, follow the instructions exactly. In all cases, observe these general guidelines.

• Whenever possible, route the water pipes in a straight line from the support equipment to the spa. Try to avoid turns, especially at 90-degree angles, so the water can flow freely and easily to the spa.

• The diameter of the pipe and fittings must remain the same for the entire distance from the support equipment to the spa. Never reduce the inside dimension of the pipe or fittings, as this will restrict the flow of water and create pressure in the line. If the water-line size is reduced, it could make the pump work harder than necessary and might even damage it.

• The support equipment must be connected to the spa in an orderly manner to avoid making a wrong juncture. Concentrate on connecting one line

at a time. Start at the support equipment and lay the line and all related fittings all the way to the spa. Do not get dirt from the trench in the pipe or fittings, as it may become trapped in the line.

• Temporarily connect all of the fittings, without cement, until you are sure everything will fit together correctly. You may have to adjust the length of a piece of pipe to get a good fit or to provide clearance for another piece of pipe. Make sure there is no strain on any of the fittings. Once a plumbing line is completely attached temporarily, and everything fits properly, its joints can be cemented as described earlier in this chapter (page 84). After one section of pipe is completed, proceed with the next section of pipe and continue until all pipes are connected.

• Use a hose-clamp fitting when attaching the air-blower pipe to the air pump. Do not use PVC solvent cement for this connection; it is highly flammable and trapped fumes from the solvent cement could ignite when the blower is turned on, causing a fire. It is safe to use PVC solvent cement in the rest of the air line, but allow it to cure for 24 hours and then allow any vapors to evaporate before starting the blower.

• After all the plumbing lines are completed, they should be pressure tested by a spa dealer or installer to make sure that all

lines are attached correctly and there is no leakage. This test requires special equipment and should be entrusted to a professional spa installer. If there is a leak in the system, it's best to find it before filling the spa with water.

Outdoor Enclosure Requirements

All heating and electrical equipment located outdoors must be protected from weather and moisture. The enclosure must be designed to allow room for servicing and for the complete removal and installation of every component located within it. If possible, design the enclosure so that it can be lifted off in one piece or in sections.

The enclosure must be properly ventilated, since the gas water heater requires fresh air for proper combustion. The amount of fresh air depends on the BTU rating of the heater—the higher the rating, the more fresh air is required. The size and type of the opening or vents will be determined by your local building code, so refer to it for these specifications.

In most cases there must be at least 6 inches of unobstructed space across the entire front of the heater, from the base of the concrete pad to the top of the heater housing. Most uninsulated heaters must be installed no closer than 6 inches from an unprotected combustible wall surface or no closer than 3 inches from a protected combustible wall surface. Most

insulated heaters must be installed no closer than 2 inches from an unprotected combustible wall surface or no closer than 1 inch from a protected combustible wall surface.

Interior Enclosure Installation

Support equipment can be installed in a residential garage if all components are protected from damage. Equipment mounted at floor level must be surrounded by adequate barriers to protect it from accidental damage in the normal path of any vehicle using the garage.

If the support equipment is mounted at floor level in a residential garage, it must be enclosed in a sealed compartment and must be accessible only from outside the garage. The heater must also receive its inlet combustible air from the exterior of the garage and must be vented to the outside with an approved chimney.

The support equipment can also be installed in a residential garage without an enclosure, provided the gas heater is mounted at least 18 inches above the floor level. This is to protect against the accidental ignition of any flammable vapors that could be present at floor level. This type of installation does not require any enclosure, but the heater must be vented to the outside with an approved chimney.

INSTALLING AN IN-GROUND SPA

Lowering a spa into an excavated hole is a heavy job, but by inviting a few good friends to help—and giving them a party afterwards—you can transform the job of installing the spa from hard labor into a social event.

How to Position the Spa

After all fittings have been attached to the spa, it is time to place it into its hole.

Reinstall the protective plastic wrap or cardboard to cover the interior surfaces of the spa shell during installation. This is important, since you will be shoveling sand into the hole and using water during this procedure.

If you have not already done so, place about 6 inches of sand into the bottom of the spa hole. Completely cover the lower surface of the hole. If the spa has a bottom drain, leave a small trench for the drain-line clearance from the drain to the side of the spa.

Placing the spa into the hole is not an easy task; you will need assistance. The number of helpers depends on how large the spa is. Never lift the spa with the plumbing pipes or fixtures, as they will be damaged and may leak. Lift the spa on level ground and practice moving it around a little. If you feel that you need additional help to safely pick up and lower the spa, round up the extra people at this time. Don't try to install the spa without sufficient help, as the spa or its plumbing may be damaged.

With the assistance of several helpers, lift the spa and carefully set it down in the hole. After the spa is lowered, check that the top rim surface is located at the correct level in relation to the surrounding ground area. If the level is incorrect, the spa must be removed and the hole adjusted to arrive at the desired level.

Once the spa is positioned correctly, level it out. Use a carpenter's level placed on a straight piece of 2 by 4 lumber or a metal angle iron that will bridge the spa from side to side. Before using either the wood or angle iron, sight down its entire length to make sure it is straight. If it is not, don't use it; it will give a false level reading. Check to be sure the spa is level in all directions. To adjust the spa, gently rock it and move it back and forth in the sand at the base of the hole.

Preliminary Backfilling

Once the spa is level in all directions, you can start backfilling the hole with sand and water. During this procedure, do not use too much water to wet the sand, as the spa could float out of position. If this happens you must start all over by removing the spa and then digging out the wet sand.

Start by shoveling sand into the hole around the perimeter of the spa up to the seat or lounge level. As the sand is shoveled into the hole, wet the sand with a garden hose only to the point at which it will flow into the voids under the spa; remember, don't use too much water.

All air spaces between the spa shell and the excavated hole must be filled with wet sand so the spa shell will be completely supported on all surfaces. Keep adding sand and water up to the seat or lounge area; continuously check to make sure the spa is still level. The spa can be adjusted slightly during the filling operation to correct the level. Make sure the sand fills all voids and is firmly packed. Correct backfilling is very important, because the spa shell must be evenly supported, especially under the floor, seating, and lounge areas. If any voids are left unfilled, unnecessary strain will be placed on the spa-shell material, which may cause stress fractures in the future.

Once the hole is filled to the seat or lounge level, stop adding sand and water.

This transit level ensures that the spa will not be tilted when it is installed. With care, a carpenter's level will provide the same results.

In-ground Spa

Decking

Concrete pad (used when soil is soft or unstable)

Sand backfill

Sturdy friends or a contractor's crew are recommended for digging the hole. For hard or rocky soil, a jackhammer may be needed.

Final Hookup and Building Inspection

At this time, connect the plumbing lines and electrical components from the spa to the support equipment. After these connections are completed, call the building department for an inspection. After the inspector has approved this phase of installation, all the water plumbing lines, natural gas pipes, and electrical systems should have passed inspection.

How to Test the Spa and the Support Equipment

Now is the time for the acid test: Will everything operate as it is supposed to? Remove the plastic wrap or cardboard that has been protecting the interior surfaces of the spa shell during installation. Thoroughly and carefully clean out any debris from inside the spa shell. Don't scratch or damage the surface while cleaning the spa. If you have installed a fiberglass spa, polish the gelcoat surface at this time, following the manufacturer's instructions.

Remove all protective plugs from all of the plumbing fixtures within the spa shell. Carefully wipe off the entire inner surface of the spa with a moist, soft cloth to remove any residual debris. The spa must be clean before adding the water because you don't want dirt in the support equipment.

After the interior of the spa is clean, fill it with fresh, cold water from a garden hose. Fill the spa to the point just above the skimmer lower level.

If a natural gas water heater is used, the gas line from the meter to the heater must be bled of all air (and any residual solvent-cement fumes, if special PVC pipe was used). Turn off the gas shutoff valve at the heater, then turn the gas main valve on. Slightly loosen the pipe-union fitting at the heater to allow all trapped air and fumes to escape from the gas line. Natural-gas pipeline pressure is very low, so it may take a while to bleed the line. When the sound of the gas escaping from the union is constant, with no pops or varying sounds, the line probably has been bled sufficiently. Tighten the pipe union at the heater. Make sure this fitting is tight. Drip soapy water on the fitting to make sure there is no gas leak (the soapy water will bubble if there is a leak). Allow any gas fumes to dissipate before turning on the water pump or lighting the water heater.

Make sure the basket is installed in the skimmer, then turn on the water pump and make sure it works. The water pump should prime itself within the first 2 minutes of operation. If the pump will not prime or is not pumping water, shut it off and call your spa dealer for assistance. Do not continue to run the pump in a dry condition, as this will damage it.

Following the manufacturer's instructions turn on all the support equipment, with the exception of a gas water heater. Let the water pump, all hydrojets, and the air blower run for 10 to 15 minutes before lighting the gas water heater. During this time, inspect all plumbing fittings and make sure there are no water leaks. If there are, correct the problem at this time. After the water pump, hydrojets, and air

95

blower have operated correctly for 15 minutes, shut them off.

At this point make sure that all electrical components are turned off. Light the water heater pilot light, following the manufacturer's instructions (some gas heaters have an electronic ignition system instead of a pilot light). After the pilot has been lighted, allow any remaining air to escape from the heater. Turn on the water heater and the water pump, and run the system until the water is heated to the desired temperature. Don't run the air blower at this time, as you want the water to heat up as fast as possible.

If any support-equipment components are not operating correctly during this test, shut down the entire system and call the spa dealer for assistance.

Final Backfilling

Reinstall the protective plastic wrap or cardboard to keep sand from falling into the spa during the final backfilling procedure. At this point you can finish backfilling the spa. Again, do not use too much water to wet the sand. Shovel the sand into the hole around the perimeter of the spa. As the sand is shoveled into the hole, wet it with the garden hose only to the point at which the sand will flow into the voids around the spa and plumbing fixtures. Check continuously to make sure the spa is still level. The spa can be moved slightly during the filling operation to level it correctly. All air spaces between the spa shell and the excavated hole must be filled with wet sand so the spa shell will be completely supported on all sides. Continue to add sand until it reaches the top rim surface of the spa. Make sure the sand fills all voids and is firmly packed. After the hole is completely filled, level off the surrounding area. At this time you can either finish the installation by installing decks and landscaping or interior decor, or you can test and chemically balance the water, as described in the fifth chapter (page 102), check the water temperature, and take that first hot soak.

Air and water lines are laid in a trench that runs to the support equipment.

Top: Back-fill the hole with a mixture of sand and water. Mix thoroughly; don't use too much water.
Bottom: Follow the manufacturer's instructions to connect piping.

INSTALLING A SPA IN A HOUSE

The procedure for installing a spa in an existing house is similar to installing a spa outdoors. However, two additional points need to be considered before starting: reinforcing the floor and foundation to carry the weight of the spa, and earthquake-proofing the area around the spa.

Reinforcement of the Floor and Foundation

If the spa is going to be placed on an existing wood-framed floor, the floor must be reinforced to carry the load, and the floor surface must be waterproof.

Structural reinforcement, which requires the advice of a qualified architect or builder, is described on page 33. Depending on the location of the spa within the room, the existing foundation may have to be reinforced. Changing a foundation is usually very expensive and should be avoided, if possible.

Earthquake Protection for a Portable Spa

If you install a portable spa indoors in an area where there is frequent earthquake activity, it's a good idea to secure the portable spa to the floor. A portable spa could move around during a strong earthquake. Contact the spa dealer or manufacturer to see if they offer any type of kit to secure the spa for this purpose. If they do not offer a kit, ask if they would suggest any specific locations on the spa that could be used for attachments to hold it down. Also, ask them if adding this

feature to your spa will void any applicable warranty for the unit.

If a kit is not available, and there is no warranty problem, remove the skirting and look at the support structure. Try to find a solid support location next to the corners where a tie-down strap or angle brace could be attached to the spa structure and to the floor. The strapping or angle brackets should be securely attached to the spa structure and to the floor. If the spa is installed on a concrete slab floor, special lag screws can be used after holes have been drilled in the floor. On a wood-framed floor, the bolts can go through the flooring and subflooring.

This drain-and-fill whirlpool tub, of acrylic reinforced with fiberglass, is designed to accommodate up to four adults.

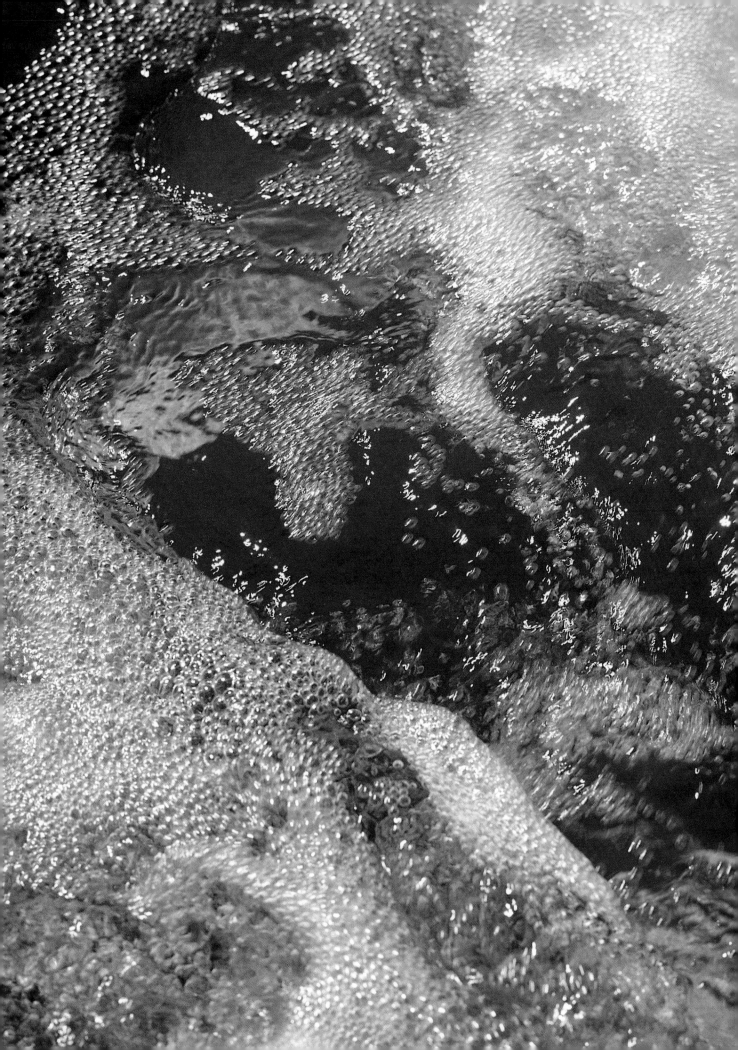

 **MAINTAINING THE SPA**

Your spa will provide years of enjoyment if it is properly maintained. Regular, simple testing and inspection will ensure that you get the most from your spa.

Spa maintenance is easy and inexpensive, and it takes relatively little time. The carefree soaking that results is well worth the effort.

This chapter will guide you through every aspect of spa maintenance, from testing the water and troubleshooting the support equipment to repairing minor problems and preparing the spa for winter.

Careful attention to the simple tasks involved in spa maintenance will keep the water healthful and inviting.

MAINTAINING THE WATER

Proper maintenance will keep the water sparkling clear and healthful. To maintain the water properly, you must know how and when to test it and which chemicals to use to keep it clean and safe. Maintaining the water properly will eliminate bacteria and guard against eye and skin irritations.

Water Chemistry

The chemistry of the spa water can change because of an increase in the temperature of the water or air as well as from normal use. The ratio of bodies to water volume is far greater in a spa than in an average-sized swimming pool, so the spa water chemistry can change rapidly. The National Spa and Pool Institute states that 5 people in a 500- to 700-gallon spa is equal to about 250 people in an average-sized swimming pool containing 25,000 gallons of water. For this reason, the condition of the water must be checked more often with a spa than with a swimming pool.

The recommended spa water temperature of 100° to 104° F (38° to 40° C) is an ideal environment for bacteria and algae. The water temperature and rapid loss of disinfectants and sanitizers through evaporation make it necessary to check and adjust the water chemistry frequently.

The spa water should be neutral; that is, neither acidic nor alkaline. Acidic and alkaline conditions are corrected with various chemicals.

Unless you are filling the spa from a well on your own property, the mineral content of the water you receive from your water supplier may vary. Some communities purchase water from various sources; for this reason, the hardness or softness of the water may change. The water company may also introduce additives into the water to keep it healthful, and in some areas fluoride might be added.

Because water composition varies, the types of chemicals and the ratio of chemicals to water used on the last fill-up may not work as well on the next fill-up. Because of these variations, spa water must always be monitored carefully and chemically treated after refilling the spa with fresh water.

Many of the spa chemical companies offer complete spa-care kits with various combinations of the chemicals and cleaners that you will need, as well as a water testing kit and thermometer. Spa dealers usually have a supply of these kits by different manufacturers and can advise you on which one would serve your needs best.

Tests on the Water

If the spa is used every day, the water chemistry should be checked daily. If the spa is not used, an every-other-day schedule will be sufficient.

The only way to test the spa water is with an accurate test kit. Some kits test the pH factor, the parts per million (ppm) of total alkalinity, and ppm of free chlorine. The best kits test these three factors as well as total hardness, cyanuric acid, and total chlorine. No matter which type of kit you use, always follow the manufacturer's instructions exactly.

One type of test kit uses strips of paper, like litmus paper, with different bands. When the strip is dipped into spa water, the bands react to the different elements of the water chemistry. After the strip has been dipped into the water, it is compared with a color chart, furnished with the test kit, to determine the acidity or alkalinity of the water.

The other type of test kit works with water samples collected from the spa in a test vial. The samples are mixed with reagents supplied with the kit, then compared with a color chart to determine water condition. If you use this type of test kit, replace the reagents once a year.

Some of the larger swimming pool and spa dealers have in-house water testing laboratories. The fees are reasonable, and it's advisable to have this type of test performed once a month to make sure you are testing the spa water correctly.

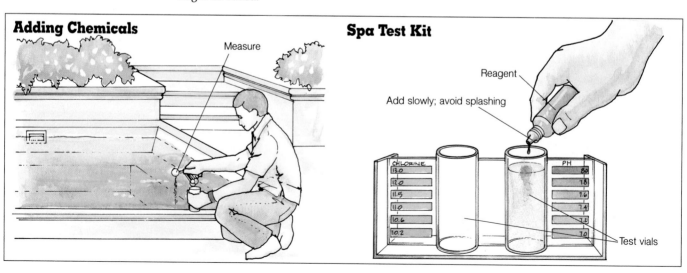

Adding Chemicals

Measure

Spa Test Kit

Reagent

Add slowly; avoid splashing

CHLORINE
13.0
12.0
11.5
11.0
10.6
10.2

PH
8.0
7.8
7.6
7.4
7.2
7.0

Test vials

Regular treatment with a sanitizing agent is important to a healthful spa. Several types are available, each with advantages and disadvantages. This section will explain the differences.

Water Circulation

Ample and consistent water circulation through the spa and support equipment is very important in maintaining healthful spa water. Make sure the skimmer basket is clear of debris. Check the antivortex cover on the drain for any debris that has sunk to the bottom. Also look for and remove accumulated hair at or near the drains.

Chlorine

Chlorine is the disinfectant preferred by swimming pool and spa owners, as well as by most pool and spa maintenance services. Chlorine kills algae and bacteria and helps oxidize solid matter in the water. It also helps to keep the water clear. Chlorine comes in various forms: gas (used mainly in large public swimming pools), liquid, granules, and in larger solid forms, such as tablets.

Ask your spa dealer to recommend a type of chlorine for your particular spa and for the water conditions in your area. If possible, choose an organic chlorine with a cyanuric acid base; it is the safest to use. This type of chlorine is identified with the words "di-chlor" or "tri-chlor" on the label. Inorganic chlorine products have a calcium base (such as calcium hypochlorite) that can be combustible when mixed with organic substances; these should be avoided. Organic-based chlorine resists deterioration caused by sunlight and is used most often in outdoor spas.

Bromine

Bromine sanitizes water in a manner similar to chlorine, but it is less popular than chlorine. Bromine is available in stick, tablet, and powder form and is used in a two-step method.

Bromine has advantages and disadvantages compared with chlorine. The advantages are that it doesn't evaporate as quickly in the hotter water used in spas; and in most cases, it doesn't irritate the eyes as chlorine does. And only in rare cases does it irritate the skin.

The disadvantages are that it is usually more expensive than chlorine and is not as stable in sunlight, which decreases its effectiveness in outdoor spas; but bromine will perform quite well indoors. It will allow chemical compounds to form if the pH level in the water is allowed to drop.

Iodine

Iodine is the least desirable of the three disinfectants discussed in this section. Iodine is used in some large swimming pools, but it must be carefully controlled. Too much iodine can discolor the water. Iodine is not generally recommended for home spa use.

Filling a Spa

Taking a Litmus Test

TREATING THE WATER

Balanced water is the single most important factor in maintaining a healthful spa. To balance the spa water, you must bring the pH level, the total alkalinity, and the calcium hardness into alignment. During routine water testing you will find out which chemical or chemicals are needed to bring the water into balance.

Initial Water Treatment

This procedure should be carried out when the spa is first installed as well as each time the spa is drained and refilled.

Ask your spa dealer how much chlorine or bromine should be added to the spa for a start-up. Add the recommended amount to the water near the center of the spa. Don't pour the chemical close to the skimmer, as it will be drawn into the pump and filter before it has mixed with the spa water. Using a clean piece of wood as a paddle, carefully and gently stir the chemicals into the water until they are evenly dispersed.

At this time, turn on the water pump and let it run for four to six hours to mix the chemicals with the water thoroughly. Turn off the water pump and test the water for calcium hardness, pH level, total alkalinity, and chlorine level, using one of the test kits described in this chapter.

Calcium Hardness

Calcium hardness is the most difficult level to reduce in most spas. Therefore, bring the calcium level into the acceptable range first, then bring the pH

and total alkalinity into phase with the calcium level.

The calcium level indicates that the water is hard, soft, or somewhere in between (the ideal range is between 150 and 400 ppm). If the calcium level is too low (as with softer water) it can corrode the plumbing pipes, the water heater, and the filter. If you have a custom-built spa made from shotcrete or cement, soft water can also damage the plaster and concrete. Never fill the spa with a garden hose that is connected to a water softener. On the other hand, too much calcium disrupts the water chemistry and can damage the plumbing pipes, the water heater, and the filter.

To raise the hardness of the water, add calcium chloride; to lower the hardness, add a sequestering agent. These chemicals are available at most spa dealers.

Maintenance of Correct pH Level

The pH level of the water indicates its acidity or alkalinity. The pH scale runs from 1.0 to 14.0. The numbers from 1.0 to 6.9 indicate an acidic condition; 7.0 indicates a neutral condition; 7.1 to 14.0 indicate an alkaline condition. The desirable pH level ranges from 7.2 to 7.8.

If the pH level is too high (above 7.8), add muriatic acid or sodium bisulfate. If the pH level is too low (below 6.9), add sodium carbonate.

Control of Alkalinity

The alkalinity, or total alkalinity, of the water refers to the amount of all alkaline compounds in the water. These include hydroxides, carbonates, bicarbonates, and all other alkaline compounds. The alkalinity of the water determines its resistance to large fluctuations in pH level. If total alkalinity is high, the pH level tends to remain high.

The main problem caused by alkalinity imbalance is the formation of scale in the spa and support system. The same chemicals that control the pH level also control the alkalinity. The alkalinity level in the water should be maintained between 80 and 150 ppm. To raise the total alkalinity, add a diluted solution of sodium bicarbonate; to lower the total alkalinity, add sodium bisulfate.

Total Dissolved Solids

Dissolved solids are always present in spas, especially in warm areas where evaporation is high. When the spa is filled with fresh tap water, it usually contains small amounts of calcium and alkaline carbonates. When the spa is used for soaking, people bring with them perspiration, hair-care products, and sometimes suntan lotion. In an outdoor spa, the small particles that enter

the water and are not trapped by the skimmer, such as dirt and landscape debris, continue to recirculate.

These particles usually stay in the spa water when the water evaporates. More water, containing more dissolved solids, is then added; as a result, the total dissolved solids become more and more concentrated. The acceptable level of total dissolved solids in the spa is 500 to 1,500 ppm; anything over 1,500 is unacceptable. When the maximum level is exceeded, the only way to rid the spa of the dissolved solids is to drain it and refill it with fresh water.

How to Drain the Water Correctly

Water drained from the spa must be disposed of properly. Consult your local environmental regulatory agency regarding spa water disposal. If there are special rules in your area, abide by them.

If your home has a septic tank and you plan to drain the spa water into it, take precautions to avoid problems within the septic-tank system. Allow the chlorine level to drop to 0.5 ppm or lower and let the water cool down to normal temperature before draining it into the system. When you drain the spa, do it gradually over a three- to five-day period. If you drain all of the water into the septic tank in a short time, it will overwhelm the system. The septic tank is not designed to accommodate that much water at one time. If you drain it all at once, the sludge within the septic tank may move out into the drain-field leach lines

Solving Water Problems

Even the most carefully maintained water will occasionally develop problems. Most problems can be solved easily by using the methods described here. If the spa water chemistry is allowed to become unbalanced, the spa will not be usable. In some instances the water chemistry will become so out of balance that the only solution is to drain the spa completely and start over with fresh water.

Eye and Skin Irritations, Allergies and Rashes

In order to eliminate possible problems in the water, the pH level must be maintained within the acceptable range of 7.2 to 7.8. Irritations and possible rashes will begin to appear if the pH level falls below 7.0 or rises above 8.4. Eye and skin irritations also will occur if the percentage of chlorine or bromine in the water is too high.

Another source of irritation and rashes can develop when the chlorine or bromine in the spa mixes with the nitrogen that is present in perspiration and in some cosmetics. This forms chloramines or bromamines that release an objectionable odor.

One way to rid the spa of this condition is to add a chemical shocking agent, available from spa dealers, to the water. This agent will oxidize the chloramines or bromamines. If this fails to solve the problem, drain the spa and start with fresh water.

Water Color and Stains

If the spa water turns color, the cause is usually excessive metal content in the water. The water color indicates the metal content.
• Green—high copper or iron content
• Red or reddish brown—rust
• Brown or black—high manganese content

The metal content may be carried in the fresh water used to fill the spa. The types and percentages of metals vary with different locations and water sources. The metals can also come from eroding metals within the support equipment, a low pH level, low alkalinity, or a low calcium level. If the

spa water takes on one of these colors, and the problem is not corrected, the inner surface of the spa may be stained or damaged. To correct the problem, first make sure the pH level in the water is within the 7.2-to-7.8 range. If the pH level is correct, add a chemical agent, available from spa dealers, to the water.

If the spa has become stained, drain the spa water, remove the stains with a spa-shell cleaner, following the instructions on the container, and refill with fresh water.

Turbidity

Turbid, or cloudy, water has several causes and remedies.
• A low percentage of chlorine or bromine in the water—add chlorine or bromine.
• Clogged water filter—clean or replace the filter.
• Water level below the lower edge of the skimmer; water not going through filter—add water to the spa.
• The pH balance is too high, above 7.8 (total alkalinity)—add muriatic acid or sodium bisulfate.

• Body oil, suntan lotion, soap residue, or other foreign matter—add a spa chemical containing organic polymers.
• An imbalance or too many conflicting spa chemicals—drain the spa and refill with fresh water.

Excessive Foaming

Excessive foaming has several causes and remedies.
• Body oil, cosmetics, suntan lotion, soap, or shampoo residue—add a spa chemical containing a nonoily silicone-based emulsion.
• The pH balance is too high, above 7.8—add muriatic acid or sodium bisulfate.

Algae

A buildup of algae in the spa water has several causes and remedies.
• A low percentage of chlorine or bromine in the water—add chlorine or bromine.
• Using a brand of chlorine or bromine that cannot control algae in your particular water—change to a different brand of chlorine or bromine.
• The pH balance is too high, above 7.8—add muriatic acid or sodium bisulfate.

and plug the holes in the pipes. If this happens, sewage may back up into the house plumbing.

Since the spa water has a chemical residue, it is considered wastewater and must be treated as such. The spa water should be drained into the house sewage system so it will

be treated before being released. Never drain the spa water into the storm-drain system, since it may find its way into a waterway in an untreated condition. Never drain the spa water in a location where it will drain into a natural waterway where fish are present, as they may be harmed.

If local regulations allow draining spa water onto a land

surface, the water must be as free of chemicals as possible. First, chlorinate the water to achieve 1.0 ppm of chlorine-residual and then let it stand until the chlorine level has dropped to 0.5 ppm or lower. Do not run the water heater during this period since the

water must be cool (at ambient room or yard temperature) when it is drained. Once the water has been chlorinated and allowed to cool, it can be drained onto the land surface (if local regulations permit).

Slowly drain the spa water onto the dirt portion of the yard. If possible, keep the water away from grass and fragile vegetation, as some plants may be harmed.

MAINTAINING SUPPORT EQUIPMENT

Properly installed support equipment is quiet and inconspicuous, but it shouldn't be ignored. A brief daily check will spot problems in their early stages, before they become difficult and expensive to fix.

Maintenance Needs

The spa and support equipment should be inspected briefly every day. Check for any leaks or abnormal noises. If a fossil-fuel heater is used, check for any odor that may indicate a gas leak. Make sure the spa cover is securely locked. These checks will take only about 5 minutes and can save a great deal of time and money. If you find a potential problem with any part of the spa, take care of it right away.

Support-equipment maintenance needs vary with each piece of equipment. All components are manufactured to different specifications and require varying types of service and maintenance. In some cases you can observe only the exterior of the unit, since taking it apart may void its warranty.

Filter Cleaning

Regular filter cleaning is one of the most important parts of support-equipment maintenance.

Most home spas are equipped with a cartridge-type filter, which is the easiest to maintain properly. Follow the manufacturer's instructions for cleaning the filter.

When the filter is removed for cleaning, thoroughly inspect the filter housing and plumbing. Look for cracks, fractures, or corrosion on the filter housing. Correct any problems as they arise to prevent more expensive ones in the future.

Water-Pump Motor

Most water-pump motors are sealed and require no routine maintenance. Electric motors must have good ventilation, free of dirt and moisture. If your support equipment is outdoors, it should be enclosed to protect it from the elements and it must also have good ventilation.

The pump motor should have adequate clearance all around it for cooling air circulation. The amount of clearance is usually specified in the manufacturer's literature; follow it exactly to avoid problems.

Some electric motors have a built-in fan that draws air in one end of the motor and pushes it over the commutator and out the other end or through vents on the sides of the housing. If your motor has this feature, make sure the air inlet and outlets are clean and free of any landscape debris that may have entered the support-equipment enclosure. This air flow is necessary to keep the motor cool.

Never store spa or landscape chemicals in the support-equipment enclosure, since vapors could be drawn into the motor and cause corrosion.

All electric motors make a certain amount of noise when they are running; this is normal. Become acquainted with this typical sound so you can tell the difference if it changes. If the motor sounds different, first check to be sure that all air inlets and outlets are clear. If the motor is noisy or abnormally hot, turn the support-equipment system off and have the motor examined.

Air Blowers

Air blowers run at a very high speed to generate the desired volume of air. This usually produces a lot of heat. As with the water-pump motor, make sure the air-blower motor has good ventilation and is free of debris.

One of the most common problems with air blowers is air pipes that are too small in diameter. Recommended minimum diameter is 2 inches. If the diameter is too small, back pressure within the system will cause motor failure.

Another common problem is water backflow from the air outlets in the spa shell, through the air lines, to the motor. The water can ruin the motor if it reaches it; even if it doesn't, it will strain the motor by making it push water out of the air line. This problem can be prevented by installing a check valve or raised loop of the type described in the fourth chapter (page 82).

Heater

Heater maintenance begins with sustaining properly balanced spa water chemistry. The spa water circulates through the heat exchanger copper tubes within the heater unit.

Chlorine is caustic; over-chlorinated water will corrode the heat exchanger tubes, eventually causing a water leak within the heater.

When you add chlorine to the spa water, be sure to mix the chemicals with the water thoroughly. Run the water pump and heater for at least 3 to 4 hours to mix the solution. If it is not mixed properly, an overchlorinated water solution may remain in the heater and damage the copper pipes.

Whenever you service any part of the support equipment, check the heater for abnormal noise, water leakage, corrosion, or any unusual appearance. If the heater is fueled by gas or oil, check for any fuel leakage and, if you find one, correct the leak immediately.

Electrical Maintenance

When working on any portion of the spa, make sure the electrical service to the spa is turned off at the main electrical panel. If there is any electrical arcing or sparking associated with the spa, turn off the electricity to the spa *immediately.* Never allow any frayed electrical cords or loose electrical connections in the vicinity of the spa where water is or could be present. Never allow water to collect on the floor or deck where electrical switches or controls are located, and never operate any type of electrical switch or appliance while standing in water—even a small amount.

Water and electricity are a deadly combination to be avoided at all times.

EQUIPMENT TROUBLESHOOTING

You can expect your spa to give you years of trouble-free pleasure. When the occasional equipment problem occurs, a resourceful do-it-yourselfer will often be able to solve it efficiently.

Support Equipment

As with maintenance, techniques for troubleshooting of support equipment vary with each piece of equipment. Support-equipment manufacturers usually provide a troubleshooting section with the technical literature that you receive from the dealer.

With any type of troubleshooting, use a systematic, methodical approach. Don't overlook the obvious, and never assume anything.

Inspect the electrical system first. If the water pump or air blower won't run, start with the electrical panel and switches. Make sure the switch is in the ON position. If it is, see if the water-pump circuit breaker has tripped and shut down its circuit. If it has tripped, reset it; if it trips again, there is probably a major problem somewhere in that circuit. Never try to jam a circuit breaker in the ON position or bypass it with a jumper wire, as you will defeat the built-in safety of the system. This could start a fire or cause a deadly electric shock. If you feel unqualified to check out the electrical circuit yourself, call a licensed electrician.

If a fossil-fuel heater does not operate, check the shutoff valve. Someone may have turned it off by mistake. If this isn't the problem, check for any loose or disconnected electrical wires leading to a thermostat or control panel. Again, if you feel unsure, call a contractor.

If the filter is not operating correctly and you have cleaned the filter according to the manufacturer's instructions, there may be a plugged water line somewhere in the system. Make sure the filter-housing inlet and outlet fittings are clear to allow free water flow.

Water-Line Leaks

After the spa has been in service for a while you may find that you are losing water beyond that lost by splashing and evaporation. The cause may be a leak in an underground pipe or fitting.

A precision leak-detection service, available in most areas of the country, can trace a water leak without disturbing the ground surface in any way. The water lines can be traced under concrete, asphalt, and cement slabs and behind walls. The leak is traced by a unique sonar system along with an ultrasound field tester.

Once the leak is detected, the spa is drained. A special sealant is then applied in a flow-coating process that seeks out the leak and seals it off. Once the sealant has cured, the spa is again refilled with water without disturbing the yard.

Handling, Storing, and Disposing of Chemicals

Chemicals serve a very important function in spa maintenance. They should be handled and stored with care.
• Read the labels and follow the directions exactly.
• Keep chemicals out of the reach of children.
• Store the chemicals in a dry, cool place that is well ventilated, and keep them off the floor to avoid drawing moisture.
• Never store spa chemicals with lawn or garden chemicals or any flammable mixtures.
• Never mix two chemicals together unless directed to do so by the chemical manufacturer.
• Always add chemicals to water—never add water to chemicals.
• Never add chemicals to the spa when people are in it.
• Do not inhale chemical fumes or chemical dust while mixing chemicals with water.
• Do not interchange lids on containers. The original lid is designed to seal its own container.
• Do not stack the chemicals on top of each other. One container may leak and drain onto another chemical, causing a reaction.
• Test-kit chemicals should be replaced every year.
• Dispose of old chemicals according to local environmental regulations.

Tips for a Safe and Healthful Spa

Spas are designed for enjoyment, but some basic commonsense rules must be followed.
• Post a set of safety rules and emergency phone numbers next to the spa. Include the street address and phone number of your residence.
• Post maximum safe-soaking times and temperatures next to the spa. The National Spa and Pool Institute recommends a maximum soaking time of 15 minutes for adults and 10 minutes for children. (Pregnant women should check with their physicians first.) Never heat the water above 104° F (40° C).
• Alcohol, drugs, and hot soaking do not mix.
• Avoid getting long hair close to the drain to prevent entanglement.
• Electricity and water do not mix. Never handle any electrical appliance, even a portable telephone, while any portion of your body is in the spa or while standing on any wet surface around the spa.
• Secure the area around outdoor spas with fencing and lockable gates.
• Always keep the spa covered and locked when people are not using it.
• If you are having a party for children as well as adults, designate a spa supervisor who can operate the support equipment and keep an eye on the children.

MAINTAINING THE SPA SURFACE

Much of the beauty of a spa comes from its interior surface. The like-new luster of the spa can be preserved with regular maintenance; minor damage can be repaired with simple do-it-yourself methods.

Surface Care

The water in an acrylic or Rovel® thermoplastic spa should be routinely drained every 3 months and the interior surface thoroughly cleaned. Fiberglass spas should be drained every 2 months and the gelcoat surface should be polished to maintain its luster. If the spa is used daily and by a lot of soakers, you should consider performing the draining and cleaning operation more often to keep the spa surface in top condition.

The surface will deteriorate just like the finish on your boat, camper shell, or car if it is not well cared for. Routine maintenance of the finish is a must if you want the spa to look great for a long time. Maintenance products formulated specifically for spa use are available from most spa dealers, and these should be used.

Drain the spa of all water, as described in this chapter (page 102), and carefully remove any residual grit and dirt that may have settled to the bottom of the spa. You don't want this dirt to get on the cloth or mix with the cleaner while you are cleaning the spa.

Use a high-quality, mild *nonabrasive* detergent or a special cleaner designed specifically for the surface material of your spa. Never use a household scouring cleanser, as it may damage the finish. Use a natural or synthetic sponge or a soft cloth (such as an old diaper) with the cleaner. Avoid using a brush, as it may slightly scratch the surface.

After you have used the cleaner, wipe off all residue with a damp cloth and rinse thoroughly. You don't want any cleaner residue in the water when the spa is refilled because it will affect the water chemistry.

After the spa surface is cleaned, it's a good idea to apply a finish coat containing a wax that will not break down when subjected to heat and chemicals. This finish coat is formulated for specific materials, so when purchasing it select one that will work on your particular spa shell—acrylic, Rovel® thermoplastic, or fiberglass.

If your spa has an inner surface made from natural materials (such as onyx, marble, or slate), consult with the spa manufacturer for maintenance procedures, since they vary dramatically. If you use the wrong product to clean these materials, the surfaces may become permanently stained.

Repairing Damaged Gelcoat Spa Surfaces

No matter how careful you are, the spa surface may be nicked or damaged in some way. Don't neglect surface damage, as it may get progressively worse if it is not repaired. This is especially true of spas made of fiberglass and gelcoat. If they are neglected, moisture will seep into the fiberglass backing and cause additional damage.

The construction of fiberglass and gelcoat spas differs from those made of acrylic or Rovel® thermoplastic. Fiberglass spas have a thin gelcoat surface (a polyester resin with a coloring agent added to it). A thicker layer of fiberglass resin and cloth is then laminated onto the backside of the gelcoat surface.

A persistent problem with this type of construction is blistering and delamination of the gelcoat surface. This causes air leaks and water seepage, resulting in costly repairs.

Gelcoat and fiberglass have been around for years and are almost universal in formulation. You can probably purchase a repair kit or supplies from a large paint-supply store or boat shop, or you may be able to get repair supplies from the spa manufacturer. The most difficult problem will be matching the color of the gelcoat, since the original gelcoat color usually fades after years of exposure.

If the damage is confined to a surface chip, gouge, or crack, you can probably repair it yourself. If the damage is severe and there is evidence of delamination resulting in damage to the fiberglass shell, it should be repaired by a professional. If you can't find a spa-shell refinisher, you may be able to find a boat-repair service that can perform the job.

For gelcoat surface repairs you will need some liquid gelcoat, color-matched to your spa, and some hardener or catalyst. If the damage continues through the gelcoat and into the fiberglass material, you will also need some short strands of fiberglass. In order to mix the gelcoat, you will need a flat mixing plate like a small piece of masonite, formica, or other similar hard-surfaced nonporous material. Don't work on a piece of porous material, as the catalyst may soak into it instead of mixing with the gelcoat. You will need a putty knife or wooden stirring stick to mix the gelcoat and catalyst. You will also need an industrial-type single-edged razor blade, a hard rubber squeegee, a rubber sanding block, 200-grit and 600-grit wet-or-dry sandpaper, some waxed paper, and polishing compound.

Follow manufacturer's instructions for the ratio of liquid gelcoat to catalyst. The ratio between these two compounds is critical to obtaining a durable hard-surfaced result. The ambient temperature and humidity on the day you are using this product also affects the curing time and hardness. It's advisable to mix a sample batch and see if it sets up properly and becomes hard—not rubbery—when it is finally cured.

Fiberglass that contacts skin may cause severe itching. To play it safe, wear a long-sleeved shirt, button it up to your neck, and tape the sleeve openings to your wrists with masking tape; wear heavy rubber gloves. You should also wear a disposable face mask while sanding, to avoid breathing any of the gelcoat dust.

The following is a basic step-by-step procedure for repairing a damaged gelcoat surface. If you purchase a repair kit, follow its instructions if they differ from those presented here.

1. Drain the spa of all water and wipe it dry.

2. Clean the damaged area and surrounding area of all residual wax and cleaner. The surface must be free of any foreign substance in order for the new gelcoat to laminate correctly to the existing gelcoat.

3. Cover the remaining spa surface to protect it from damage, since you will probably be sitting and working within the spa. Take off your shoes or wear tennis shoes.

4. Remove any chipped or peeling gelcoat from around the damaged area.

5. If the gouge is deep, use an electric drill with a drill bit or burr to roughen the gouge so the patch will stick. Blow out all residue.

6. Use 200-grit wet-or-dry sandpaper and carefully roughen the area surrounding the gouge by about 1 inch in all directions. Wipe off the entire area, as it must be clean, dry, and free of any debris.

7. If the damage continues into the fiberglass, follow the steps below before continuing to repair the gelcoat.

a. Place some gelcoat and catalyst on a plate and mix it thoroughly with a putty knife or flat wooden stirring stick. Use a slow back-and-forth motion to mix the two elements. Don't stir and don't mix too fast, or you will introduce small air bubbles into the mixture.

b. After the gelcoat and catalyst are thoroughly mixed, slowly add pieces of fiberglass fibers into the mixture. Make sure all fibers are thoroughly saturated with the liquid.

c. Slowly work this compound into the damaged hole with the point of a knife or small screwdriver. This material must be pushed into all of the nooks and crannies of the damaged area. Any air pockets will create future problems. Fill the area to a level slightly above the surrounding surface. Do not leave an excessive amount, as it will have to be removed later when it is partially hardened.

d. Place a piece of waxed paper over this patch and smooth out the top surface with the backside of the single-edged razor blade. Leave the waxed paper in place for about 10 minutes. During this time the patch will become hot due to the chemical reaction between the gelcoat and the catalyst; this is normal.

e. Remove the waxed paper. The patch should be partially cured by this time and it should feel slightly hard.

f. Using a sharp single-edged razor blade, carefully trim off the top surface of the patch so it is flush with the surrounding area.

g. Allow the patch to cure thoroughly. The curing time will vary due to differences in air temperature and humidity. When thoroughly cured, the patch must be as hard as the surrounding surface and will have shrunk until it is lower than the surrounding area.

h. Use 100-grit wet-or-dry sandpaper and carefully roughen the patch so the next

layer will have something to adhere to.

8. Place some gelcoat and catalyst on a plate and mix it thoroughly with a putty knife or flat wooden stirring stick. Mix in a slow back-and-forth motion. Don't stir and don't mix too fast, or you will introduce small air bubbles into the mixture.

9. Slowly work this compound into the slight depression or partially patched hole. Use a putty knife and apply the mixture slowly to the area. Avoid trapping air bubbles because they will show when the patch is completed. Do not leave an excessive amount of the gelcoat mixture on the surface, as it will have to be removed later when it is partially hardened.

10. Place a piece of waxed paper over this patch and smooth out the top surface with the backside of the single-edged razor blade. Leave waxed paper in place for about 10 minutes. During this time the patch will become hot due to the chemical reaction between the gelcoat and the catalyst; this is normal.

11. Remove the waxed paper. The patch should be partially cured by this time and it should feel slightly hard.

12. Using a sharp single-edged razor blade, carefully trim off the top surface of the patch so it is flush with the surrounding area. After you have trimmed off the top surface, there will be some small bubble holes in the gelcoat. This is normal, no matter how hard you try to avoid them.

13. Again, mix a very small amount of gelcoat and catalyst. Mix it *very, very slowly* so there are no air bubbles this time.

14. Apply this mixture to one side of the patch and place a piece of waxed paper over the gelcoat and the patch.

15. Using a hard rubber squeegee, slowly spread the gelcoat over the patch area to fill in all of the small holes in the patch and make it level with the surrounding surface. Leave the waxed paper in place for about ½ hour.

16. Allow the patch to cure thoroughly. If possible, allow it to cure overnight. When thoroughly cured it must be as hard as the surrounding area.

17. Remove the waxed paper from the surface.

18. Using a hard rubber sanding block and 600-grit wet-or-dry sandpaper, carefully sand the patch until it is even with the surrounding area.

19. Using white polishing compound and a clean cloth, buff the area of the patch to remove the small scratches caused by the sandpaper.

Repairing Damaged Acrylic or Rovel® Thermoplastic Spa Surfaces

Acrylic and Rovel® thermoplastic spas are made from a single sheet of thick plastic. The color completely permeates the material. Acrylic spas are usually backed with a layer of fiberglass resin and cloth for added strength.

Acrylic and Rovel® thermoplastic surfaces are less susceptible to damage than gelcoat. They can be repaired with a special touch-up kit, available from the spa manufacturer.

WINTERIZING THE SPA

Your spa need not be a seasonal pleasure; simple techniques can make it usable the year around. But whether you use the spa during the winter or not, you should prepare it for the cold.

There are several ways of winterizing an outdoor spa. If you are the rugged type, you can leave the spa as is and enjoy the warm bubbling water in the cold outdoors. If you are a little less stalwart, you can add a portable heavy vinyl dome cover over the spa to keep the cold air out and the warm air in and use the spa all winter long. Vinyl dome covers are supported by internal air pressure generated by a special electric fan. When winter is over, you simply remove the dome cover and store it until next winter.

If you live in an area where winter temperatures fall below freezing, you should insulate the spa, the plumbing, and the support equipment, as described in the fourth chapter (page 88). It may be best to leave the spa filled with water or to drain it partially during the cold winter months. This depends on how cold it gets in your area, the type and construction of your spa, and how well everything is insulated. Because of these variables, consult with your spa dealer. You may also want to talk to several swimming pool maintenance companies; because of their experience, they can often give you expert advice.

If this is your first winter with a new spa, it's advisable to have a spa or swimming pool maintenance company winterize the spa the first time. You can observe them and ask why they are doing certain things. Make notes; then next winter you can do it yourself.

If the spa remains filled with water in subfreezing weather, you can use automatic timers and special controls to circulate the water through the entire water system to keep the water from freezing. However, don't use the heater to maintain a spa temperature below 70° F. Some systems are controlled by a time clock; others take water and ambient air temperature readings and turn on the support equipment when it is necessary.

If the support-equipment enclosure is outside, it must be insulated, but there also must be enough air flow to keep the pump motor from overheating. If the housing is attached to the house, you may be able to pump some of the warm air from the house into the enclosure.

For in-ground spas, if you do choose to empty the spa, consult your spa dealer or a maintenance company in your area. If you drain the spa, drain only about half the water. If all of the water is evacuated, the spa will be pushed up out of the ground due to hydrostatic pressure of the soil. Wet or frozen soil exerts most of its pressure against the top portion of the spa walls and can cause them to buckle or crack.

If you have a wooden hot tub, do not empty it, as it will be permanently damaged. If the tub is drained, the wooden staves will shrink away from each other, the metal bands or hoops will slide down the staves, and you will end up with an expensive pile of firewood. Once a wooden tub has dried out, it cannot be salvaged. The hot tub must have water in it at all times, even in freezing weather. Protect it accordingly.

Rigid Spa Cover

Rigid cover

GLOSSARY

Acidity The pH level in the water is in the 1.0-to-6.9 range. Prohibits removal of suspended materials in the spa water. Can cause corrosion in plumbing and support equipment.

Algae Tiny plantlike living organisms that grow in water and cling to the sides of the spa. They discolor the water and stain spa surfaces.

Algicide A chemical agent used to kill algae on contact.

Alkalinity The property of water formed primarily by soluble salts—bicarbonates, carbonates, and hydroxides. Indicated by a pH level of 7.1 to 14.0.

Bacteria Minute unicellular organisms of various forms. Some can cause disease.

Baking soda See *Sodium bicarbonate.*

Balanced water Balanced water is properly adjusted in all aspects of its chemical content, including pH level, total alkalinity, calcium hardness, and total dissolved solids.

Bromine A chemical disinfectant used to sanitize and purify water. Kills algae and bacteria and oxidizes suspended dirt particles in the spa water. Available in stick, tablet, and powder form.

Calcium chloride A white chemical powder used to raise the calcium level in the water.

Calcium hardness The term used to indicate the mineral content of the water.

Cartridge filter A type of filter made of treated paper of either Dacron or nonwoven polyester that is accordion-pleated and capped at each end. It traps dirt before the water enters the pump and heater.

Chlorinator A device that adds chlorine to the water at a controlled rate.

Chlorine A chemical disinfectant used to sanitize and purify water. Kills algae and bacteria and oxidizes suspended dirt particles in the spa water. Chlorine is available in liquid, granular, tablet, and coarse powder form.

Chlorine-residual The amount of chlorine available for sanitizing the water after the initial chlorine demand of the water has been reached.

Cyanuric acid A chemical added to the water to retard the loss of chlorine from sunshine.

Filter rate The speed and volume of water through the spa filter. Rated in gallons of flow per minute per square foot of effective filtration area.

GFCI (Ground Fault Circuit Interrupter) A special electrical outlet or circuit breaker that deadens the outlet or circuit whenever there is a potential for electrical shock.

Gunite Method of constructing a free-form in-ground spa with concrete applied through high-pressure hoses over reinforcement bars.

Hardness The amount of calcium and magnesium dissolved in the water. The water is neutral, hard, or soft. If the water is other than neutral, it can damage the spa and the support-equipment components.

Iodine A chemical disinfectant, either potassium or sodium iodine, used as a germicide to purify the spa water.

Muriatic acid A form of hydrochloric acid used to lower the pH factor of the water.

pH The relative degree of acidity or alkalinity of the spa water by hydrogen ion concentration. The pH scale ranges from 1.0 to 14.0, with an ideal range for spas of 7.2 to 7.8.

Potable water Water which is bacteriologically safe and approved for human consumption (safe for drinking).

ppm Indicates the parts per million of a certain element within the water, for example: 10 ppm of salt equals 10 parts of salt per million parts of water in the spa.

Recirculating system The closed-loop system that recirculates spa water.

Scale Deposits of waterborne minerals that stick to spa walls and inner parts of support equipment.

Shock treatment The addition of spa chemicals to the spa water in quantities greater than normal to eliminate or control a specific problem.

Shotcrete See *Gunite.*

Skimmer A device on the side of the spa where the water exits the spa to go to the support equipment. It catches floating debris, preventing it from entering the filter, pump, and water heater.

Soda ash A dry chemical used to increase the pH level (raise the alkalinity) of the spa water.

Sodium bicarbonate A chemical used to raise the alkalinity of the spa water.

Sodium bisulfate A chemical compound of sodium and acid sulfide used to lower the pH level of the spa water (increase its acidity).

Stabilization The addition of greater-than-normal amounts of chlorine when there is excessive heat, abnormal rainfall, or heavy spa use. This converts the chlorine into free available chlorine by destroying the ammonia in the spa water.

Total alkalinity The total measured amount of all alkaline chemicals in the spa water.

Turnover rate The time required to completely circulate the volume of water through the filtration and heating system.

Weir The small hinged gate in the opening of the skimmer. Its construction controls the rate at which water is allowed to enter the skimmer.

INDEX

U.S./Metric Measure Conversion Chart

		Formulas for Exact Measures			**Rounded Measures for Quick Reference**		
	Symbol	**When you know:**	**Multiply by:**	**To find:**			
Mass (Weight)	oz	ounces	28.35	grams	1 oz		= 30 g
	lb	pounds	0.45	kilograms	4 oz		= 115 g
	g	grams	0.035	ounces	8 oz		= 225 g
	kg	kilograms	2.2	pounds	16 oz	= 1 lb	= 450 g
					32 oz	= 2 lb	= 900 g
					36 oz	= 2¼ lb	= 1000 g (1 kg)
Volume	tsp	teaspoons	5.0	milliliters	¼ tsp	= 1/24 oz	= 1 ml
	tbsp	tablespoons	15.0	milliliters	½ tsp	= 1/12 oz	= 2 ml
	fl oz	fluid ounces	29.57	milliliters	1 tsp	= 1/6 oz	= 5 ml
	c	cups	0.24	liters	1 tbsp	= ½ oz	= 15 ml
	pt	pints	0.47	liters	1 c	= 8 oz	= 250 ml
	qt	quarts	0.95	liters	2 c (1 pt)	= 16 oz	= 500 ml
	gal	gallons	3.785	liters	4 c (1 qt)	= 32 oz	= 1 liter
	ml	milliliters	0.034	fluid ounces	4 qt (1 gal)	= 128 oz	= 3¾ liter
Length	in.	inches	2.54	centimeters	⅜ in.	= 1 cm	
	ft	feet	30.48	centimeters	1 in.	= 2.5 cm	
	yd	yards	0.9144	meters	2 in.	= 5 cm	
	mi	miles	1.609	kilometers	2½ in.	= 6.5 cm	
	km	kilometers	0.621	miles	12 in. (1 ft)	= 30 cm	
	m	meters	1.094	yards	1 yd	= 90 cm	
	cm	centimeters	0.39	inches	100 ft	= 30 m	
					1 mi	= 1.6 km	
Temperature	° F	Fahrenheit	5/9 (after subtracting 32)	Celsius	32° F	= 0° C	
					68°F	= 20°C	
	° C	Celsius	9/5 (then add 32)	Fahrenheit	212° F	= 100° C	
Area	in.^{2}	square inches	6.452	square centimeters	1 in.^{2}	= 6.5 cm^2	
	ft^2	square feet	929.0	square centimeters	1 ft^2	= 930 cm^2	
	yd^2	square yards	8361.0	square centimeters	1 yd^2	= 8360 cm^2	
	a.	acres	0.4047	hectares	1 a.	= 4050 m^2	